BUFFY SAINTE-MARIE:

IT'S MY WAY

BUFFY SAINTE-MARIE:

IT'S MY WAY

BLAIR STONECHILD

FIFTH
HOUSE

Published in Canada by Fifth House Ltd.
195 Allstate Parkway
Markham, ON L3R 4T8
www.fifthhousepublishers.ca

Published in the United States by Fifth House Ltd.
311 Washington Street, Brighton, Massachusetts 02135

Library and Archives Canada Cataloguing in Publication
Stonechild, Blair
Buffy Sainte-Marie : It's my way / Blair Stonechild.
ISBN 978-1-897252-78-9
1. Sainte-Marie, Buffy. 2. Singers—Canada—Biography.
3. Composers—Canada—Biography. I. Title.
ML420.S155S88 2010   782.42164092   C2010-904578-5

Publisher Cataloging-in-Publication Data (U.S)
Stonechild, Blair.
Buffy Sainte-Marie : it's my way / Blair Stonechild.
[296] p. : photos. ; cm.
ISBN-13: 978-1-89725-278-9
1. Sainte-Marie, Buffy. 2. Singers--Canada—Biography. 3. Composers--Canada—Biography. I. Title.
782.42164092 dc22   ML420.S155S78 2010

Fifth House Ltd. acknowledges with thanks the Canada Council for the Arts, and the Ontario Arts
Council for their support of our publishing program. We acknowledge the financial support of the
Government of Canada through the Canada Book Fund (CBF) for our publishing activities.

ONTARIO ARTS COUNCIL
CONSEIL DES ARTS DE L'ONTARIO

Canada Council   Conseil des Arts
for the Arts   du Canada

Every reasonable effort has been made to contact copyright holders of images and lyrics.
The publishers would be pleased to have errors or omissions brought to their attention.

Text and cover design by Tanya Montini
Printed in Canada
10 9 8 7 6 5 4 3 2 1

Dedicated to
my mother Lucy, for her nurturing
and my soul mate Sylvia,
who continually inspires me

Last, but not least, thank you to my family for their love and patience.

Special acknowledgement goes to CineFocus–Paquin Pictures who shared their invaluable extensive archive of interviews and research developed for *Buffy Sainte-Marie: A Multimedia Life*. CineFocus Canada producers John Bessai and Joan Prowse (also the documentary's director) spent long hours and expended significant resources in obtaining the interviews. Acknowledgement of material used is seen in references throughout the book. Joan Prowse was most generous in facilitating access to these materials. Without the assistance provided by CineFocus–Paquin Pictures, this biography would not have been possible.

CineFocus Canada is a Toronto-based producer of prime-time television programs, documentaries, and educational videos in both French and English. Examples of recent projects include *Lucky Breaks*, a 26-episode television series profiling career breakthroughs by renowned Canadian and international personalities; *Museum Maestros*, about the work of Gail and Barry Lord in innovative cultural centres around the world; *Visions of the Wilderness: The Art of Paul Kane,* about the paradoxical life of the portrait artist; and *Green Heroes*, a series of stories about crusaders for the environment. An interactive Web site accompanies *Green Heroes* to extend the experience of the viewers. CineFocus has created quality, cost-effective products for numerous clients since 1991, and has won national and international acclaim and awards for its work.

Paquin Entertainment Group is based in Winnipeg and Toronto and undertakes a variety of activities including representing artists such as Randy Bachman, Buffy Sainte-Marie, Bachman and Turner, The Sadies, The Sheepdogs, Whitehorse, Tegan and Sarah, K'NAAN, and Serena Ryder. Artist management includes arranging appearances, recording, touring, publishing, and organizing events of all sizes. In addition, the Entertainment Group has produced several feature-length films, television, and theatre productions.

INTRODUCTION

Like many Native university students in the late 1960s and early 1970s, I listened to and was inspired by the songs of Buffy Sainte-Marie. I was stirred by the lyrics of songs such as "Now That the Buffalo's Gone," and "My Country 'Tis of Thy People You're Dying," which somehow rekindled a dormant sense of pride and encouraged us as social activists, struggling to gain greater recognition of Native American issues. "Universal Soldier" was a powerful anthem of the antiwar statement of the times.

Part of a talented generation that includes Bob Dylan, Joni Mitchell, Leonard Cohen, and Joan Baez, Buffy established herself as a songwriter, singer, and pioneer of folk music. However, Buffy has also blazed off into other areas, including social activism, acting, script-writing, motherhood, digital artistry, and utilizing the Internet to reach Indigenous youth far-flung across the globe. Today Buffy continues with intense energy and commitment to pursue an active career and, in the process, is amassing an impressive legacy.

Tracking the strands of, and understanding, Buffy's complex and multidimensional life has made writing her biography quite a challenge. It was decided that the biography would be best organized along thematic lines, rather than in a strictly chronological format, to most effectively highlight her contributions and their significance. To get Buffy's full story, I spoke to many individuals of diverse backgrounds whose lives have been touched by this remarkable woman.

Buffy has made so many creative and public contributions over the past five decades that it is impossible to document everything. I apologize in advance to anyone I may have inadvertently overlooked. My main objective has been to convey a sense of who Buffy is and to reveal the drama and richness of her life. Today Buffy continues to have a tremendous impact.

In early 2010, Buffy asked her agency, Paquin Entertainment, to set up open auditions in Winnipeg to find backup musicians for her world tour to promote her eighteenth album, *Running for the Drum*. The album is diverse and replete with her trademark techno powwow—the throbbing rhythms infused with Aboriginal phrases and chants she originally introduced in 1976 as "powwow rock." When the call went out for auditions, the three-member heavy-metal band called Gathering of Flies auditioned. Buffy was looking for players who could handle the wide range of styles on *Running for the Drum* and her classic songs: love songs, rockabilly, country songs, and big rockers.

The band—Jesse Green (Lakota/Ojibwe) on guitar and vocals,

Leroy Constant (Cree) on bass and vocals, and Mike Bruyere (Ojibwe) on drums and vocals—performed three songs in its preferred heavy-metal style and Buffy recognized the group's potential immediately. That Bruyere also sang powwow was a huge plus. They played with passion, and all of them had been raised in the Aboriginal atmosphere that many of Buffy's songs originated. It was a perfect fit.

Green and the band were exhilarated to be selected as Buffy's backup on her 2010/2011 world tour. They hadn't known a lot about Buffy other than that she was a pioneer of folk music. They had seen her perform on television, knew she was interesting, educated, and influential, and that everybody loved her. She was definitely "high on the ladder" and somebody worth knowing.

The band began playing smaller venues with Buffy in Manitoba, but by mid-2010 they were headed off to exciting international destinations, including New York, Los Angeles, London, and Paris, not to mention Holland, Berlin, Brussels, Norway, and Denmark. In 2011, Buffy and the band travelled to Sydney and Melbourne in Australia, back again to Europe, and crossed Canada and the U.S.

The band was impressed by Buffy's stamina. When they were out of breath from hauling equipment up three flights of stairs, Buffy had already gathered her gear and was playing a tune at the piano. The experience proved to be an eye-opener for this new generation of Aboriginal musicians, and they enthusiastically continue to learn the secrets of musical success from one of the masters in the field.

CHAPTER 1

ALONE IN THE WOODS

On a cold, snow-swept day in February 1941, a baby girl of Cree heritage was born in the prairie town of Craven, Saskatchewan, near the poverty-stricken Piapot Indian Reserve. She had no birth certificate, but was not the only member of her community without one. Record keeping then was far from perfect, and a fire in the 1940s destroyed any local government records that then existed for the reserve. It has been impossible to locate definitive information on Buffy Sainte-Marie's earliest days; however, several stories are told about her origins.

Families on Indian reserves around Saskatchewan were extremely poor. One story suggests that, when Buffy's mother died unexpectedly after giving birth, her father was left alone to care for the newborn. Another story says that Buffy's mother had to travel to Edmonton, Alberta, and died there, leaving the baby back home with relatives on the reserve. In any case, a local missionary recommended to Buffy's father that he adopt out his infant daughter in the belief that she would have a better chance of survival with a white family. Social and religious workers of the 1940s thought the future for Indians was bleak and that their only salvation lay in assimilating into white society. Buffy was sent east to New England, with the help of church charities set up precisely for facilitating such adoptions.

Albert C. and Winifred Kenrick St. Marie, of North Reading, Massachusetts, had recently lost an infant son and hoped adoption would fill the void. While far apart geographically, connections between Saskatchewan and New England were not unknown. Father Gravel, founder of Gravelbourg, Saskatchewan, spent a decade recruiting settlers from the New England area, including several from Massachusetts. Moreover, the St. Maries had some Aboriginal background, tracing their Micmac roots back to Acadia. The infant was given the name Beverly Jean.[1]

"I may have been born in Saskatchewan to parents I never knew. I was told I was adopted and I didn't like it and I always felt insecure as a kid. I may have been orphaned or maybe not but I was brought up by a family who are part Micmac and part non-Indian in Massachusetts and in Maine. They had a trailer in Maine, by a lake in a very woodsy, foresty place, and they worked, my father as a mechanic in Massachusetts, my mother at a newspaper."[2]

Dr. Martha Henry, director of the Center for Adoption Research at the University of Massachusetts Medical School in Boston, describes typical adoptive attitudes and procedures of the 1940s and 1950s. She notes that it was not uncommon for Canadian Aboriginal children to be adopted by Massachusetts families.

"There could be a situation where someone desired a child … but couldn't have a child, or had one that died. There was a sense that they would be 'saving' the Aboriginal child."[3] Most adoption advisors believed that adopting a child from far away was beneficial to the adoptive process because geographical distance eliminated the possibility of future contact with the child's original family. Priests and doctors advised biological relatives to forget about any child given up for adoption.

Adoption arrangements were typically made through church-connected charities. A nun in one location, discovering a local family's desire to adopt, would work her network of contacts to find an available child in another location. A deal would be struck, one so informal it could be completed without paperwork or involvement from government (which, during the Second World War, had more pressing priorities). The adoption process was deliberately secretive and advice given to adopters by authority figures—be they priests, doctors, or other professionals—was not to attract attention to the adoption, but instead to incorporate the adopted child as a natural part of his or her new family as seamlessly as possible. Some authorities even created birth certificates to substantiate this process. It was taboo to speak openly about the fact of adoption. Its stigma was considered so great that it could jeopardize the well-being of both family and adoptee.

Some adoptees realized they were different by simply looking at themselves in the mirror. Others never questioned their new status, even when they looked markedly different from their new parents. It was not until many years later that social workers realized how difficult it was for a child to be placed in such racially and socially different circumstances. Some kids sensed right away, however, that a part of their identity was being denied.

Buffy grew up in Naples, Maine, and North Reading and Wakefield, Massachusetts. Today, Wakefield is a town of about 25,000, approximately twenty-four km (15 mi.) north of Boston. The town was first settled in 1638 when seven houses were built along the shores of Lake Quannapowitt, a Saugus Indian word meaning "great pond." It was a farming community whose people took advantage of the bounty of wild pigeons and turkeys, fish, grapes, blackberries, and blueberries. In 1671, settlers built a garrison house, and by 1686 had "bought" the land from the Saugus.

Wakefield remained rural and isolated until the Boston and Maine Railroad came through town in 1845. The change was dramatic. Soon the area's population doubled from 1,600 to 3,200. Rail service gave new life to existing industries, such as the shoe industry, and helped create new ones, such as ice harvesting from the lakes. Local entrepreneur Cyrus Wakefield established two companies: the Boston and Maine Foundry Company and the phenomenally successful Wakefield Rattan Company—which popularized the use of wicker furniture in the United States and gave the town its name. Wakefield celebrated its 350th anniversary in 1994.[4]

Some of Winifred Kenrick St. Marie's maternal ancestors came to Massachusetts via a circuitous route. In the 1700s, the

English prevailed in a power struggle for control of Nova Scotia, resulting in the forcible eviction of a number of the region's French occupants. In 1769 a number of English families from Cape Cod travelled north to bid on and buy what were essentially entire towns in Nova Scotia. The Kenricks were probably one of many families that immigrated to Barrington, Nova Scotia—the traditional territory of the Micmac Indians. Buffy's paternal great-grandfather, William, was born in Nova Scotia in 1800, although he elected to move to Boston as a young man. This may be how the Micmac bloodline was introduced into the Kenrick family. Grandmother Elizabeth Kenrick, who was good at spinning tales, always maintained that there was an Indian connection.

Winifred Irene Kenrick, whom Buffy called Mom, was born in Malden, Massachusetts in 1918, the youngest of eight siblings. Her father, Frank Webster Kenrick, died when she was just two years old, the result of an accidental blow to the head while working at a ship construction site. The family was left in poverty. Winifred's mother, Elizabeth, took the only job she could find, scrubbing floors in business offices in Boston. She also took in laundry and sewing. Elizabeth was strict when it came to schooling and, as a result, Winifred was able to skip two grades and graduate from high school in 1936 at the age of sixteen. She married Albert Santamaria that same year.

The Santamarias' oldest child, Alan, was born in 1936. Their second child, Wayne, died of Sudden Infant Death Syndrome at four months of age in 1940. The following year, Beverly Jean

(Buffy) was brought into the family. Winifred's third and youngest child, Elaine, was born in 1948.[5]

Buffy's sister Elaine is a petite woman with brown hair whose accent reminds you of Buffy. She and her husband, Richard, live in a second-floor apartment in a suburb northwest of Boston. Elaine remembers that her original family name was Santamaria and that her parents changed the name to St. Marie because of the anti-Italian prejudice that developed during the Second World War. In the 1960s, when Buffy became famous and controversial for her stand on Native rights and the Vietnam War, she used the French spelling, Sainte-Marie, in order to shield her family from possible repercussions against her activism.

By 1942 the family had saved enough to make the payments on a house at 24A Prospect Street, on the outskirts of downtown Wakefield. Buffy was one year old when they moved. Albert, a refrigerator mechanic, retrofitted their new house with plumbing and heating. His hobby was hunting and he would often return home with pheasants, ducks, and occasionally a deer, for the family table.[6]

The St. Maries' small house at the base of Prospect Street stood in the shadow of larger homes, each of which seemed to grow larger in size the farther up the hill one went. Buffy's friend Janice Murphy (later Palumbo) remembers the house as older and not at all fancy, with a porch in front. You walked through the front door into the living room. A piano and chairs stood on the left and on the right were the kitchen and dining area. A flight of stairs led to the second floor, with three bedrooms and a bathroom. Buffy remembers how much she enjoyed playing with and hugging a stuffed moose head that lay, unmounted, on the front porch. Thick woods abounded behind the house and Buffy remembers spending much time playing there, alone.

Many houses in the 1940s had wood stoves. Janice remembers winters in Wakefield when she and Buffy would slide down the hill near the school dressed in warm wool clothes. When Lake Quannapowitt froze over, the girls went ice skating there or at a smaller out-of-the-way pond. They stayed out for hours at a time, finally coming in to warm their feet by the oven door.

Janice doesn't remember Buffy's father well because Albert, like many other men of his generation, was the primary breadwinner and seemed to spend more time at work than at home. She does, however, recall Buffy's mother as brilliant, despite the fact that she never received a college degree. Winifred worked as a proofreader at the *Daily Item*, Wakefield's local newspaper, from 1948 until about 1954, at a time when it was rare for women to have "professional" careers. Later in her life, Winifred worked as a proofreader and copy-editor for Boston's leading educational publishing houses, Houghton Mifflin and Addison–Wesley. She was not a social person, did not belong to church or ladies' groups, was somewhat shy of people, and happy to spend her free time alone with a good novel. Buffy shares her mother's quiet disposition.

Buffy never played with dolls or joined sports teams—she loved animals. The St. Marie home housed, at various times, a dog, a cat, and lots of pet rabbits. Some of Buffy's favourite times, however, were those spent at Uncle Ed and Aunt Hazel's (her mother's relatives) farm in North Reading, Massachusetts—really just a few acres with a garden, some pigs, a cat and dog, and a few goats. Buffy loved goats, and she often gazed longingly through the fence at a neighbour's riding horses.

Buffy's love of animals notwithstanding, even at the early age of three, her main curiosity was about music. She seemed particularly attracted to the family piano that stood in a corner of the Wakefield house. Mimicking what she had seen adults do, Buffy would sit on the bench and tap the piano keys to see how they sounded. She was mesmerized by the result. Buffy says she has always heard music in her head, but when she discovered the piano her world changed. Suddenly she could express externally the sounds she heard in her mind. Playing the piano became an important outlet for her feelings, and Buffy says today she probably would have died without it. She took every opportunity to experiment with making music and the piano became her favourite toy.

Very early on, Buffy began to compose her own tunes on the piano. She had no lessons and could not read music. Instead, she figured out the composing process as natural musicians have always done—by ear. Recognizing Buffy's interest, Winifred sought out a piano teacher who was astounded at how well the young child could play. The teacher advised Winifred not to force Buffy to take music lessons unless she begged for them.

Buffy remembers her school music class as terribly frustrating and having little to do with music as she experienced it. Even at this early stage in her life, Buffy loved the gift of inner music and it meant the world to her—music was both her friend and her consolation. Disinterested in music lessons, Buffy relied on her ear and her heart to play the music in her head.[7] In solitude and in the arts she found comfort from the intolerable bullying of school and home.

"I was raised in a situation where certain family members didn't welcome me and others did. There were pedophiles in the neighbourhood, in the family, and in the house," says Buffy.[8] Janice remembers one of Buffy's older siblings as "a person who liked to hurt things to see them squirm."[9] Winifred did not realize what was happening. The abuse is not something Buffy likes to dwell on but says that, if it weren't for Winifred, she doesn't think she would have survived.

"If [my mom] had known, it probably would have even been more difficult. But she really didn't know what was going on— she didn't realize ... If you are alone and isolated and scared of someone in the house, someone in the neighbourhood, somebody in the family, and don't figure things out rationally as a child, you do what feels good. And what felt good to me was to stay home, hide from the bad guys, and play the piano ... So I grew up as kind of a child on my own. Music and art were my playmates. If things were going on in my life, happy or sad, chances are I would sit down and do something artistic. Because that was fun![10]

"As a little kid, I was a real Mrs. Mouse. I was timid and scared and terrified because I was getting knocked around a lot. I kept my mouth shut—at home, in school, and in the neighbourhood. I was a real loner. I just played my music, but one day in your life you get tired of living like that. So in my teens I cut myself off from all the negativity I had experienced. I turned my back on bitterness. If I couldn't change the old world, I could help create a new one. And for some reason it worked for me. I started to live in the future.[11]

"The part of that story I talk about is the part that I think I can use as medicine to help other kids or other families. And there is value in that, in being able to share. But when it comes to my childhood, I believe that when a young child is abused at home and feels unwelcome and is victimized, the child doesn't realize they have been victimized, she's just scared all the time. Lied to, bullied, and humiliated by older people, abused kids just develop the habits of prey. And I think that by the time I was going to school, I knew I was a loser and knew I was prey to other kids. I was younger and smaller than the other kids in my school classes. Other kids in the neighbourhood used to hitch me up with ropes like a horse and run me around.

"It wasn't so much because I was visually different as because I was psychologically different. And that's the part that was so traumatic. I wasn't raised in a neighbourhood where there were a lot of creative people like me. It wasn't appreciated ... I knew I was an artist ... I knew I made music, but I didn't value it in any kind of outward way, except as personal solace and fun. I knew I could do it at any time about any subject, and really enjoy it."[12]

The piano was Buffy's solace but it was a thing of torment for Buffy's blond, blue-eyed older brother, Alan, who actually took piano lessons and hated it. Although Buffy's father once played trumpet in a band, and her aunt and uncle enjoyed playing music privately, the music Buffy most recalls hearing in her home was that from the family phonograph:

"We had a really bad record player when I was little. The speed was all right but the needle was terrible. You could hardly even hear it. When my mom went out, I'd sneak out the vacuum cleaner. I put the vacuum pipes from the record player to my ears like earphones. We had only a few records, like Tchaikovsky's *Swan Lake*, which I listened to over and over.

"I sang in my heart. I'd hear songs in my head. I'd *hear* songs—I didn't write songs. And they were always different. It was like I had a radio playing. One time I was nodding my head in time to the music. When my mom asked what I was doing, I told her I was keeping time in my head. I felt this was a built-in connection to the Creator and it worked. From the start I just took it for granted. I guess that was fortunate, because most people are conditioned against it. But I also feel that music is completely natural, because every tribe of natural people has known it. As far back as I can remember, I talked to the Creator and He talked back, and it was similar to hearing music in my head. I doubted my own identity, because people told me that there were no Indians, that the

Indians in cowboy movies were really white people. I doubted all things but music and prayer."[13]

Winifred's brothers and sisters occasionally talked about being part Micmac. Most people in those days had never heard about the Micmac (Mi'kmaq) First Nation in Nova Scotia. Cherokee, Sioux, or Navajo were familiar, but the Micmac seemed somewhat obscure by comparison. "In many ways we were not treated well in the family or in town. We were working-class in a town of blond butterflies and we didn't really have any social connections. In New England you didn't talk much about anything Native. It just seemed irrelevant."[14]

Winifred was caring and concerned about her daughter, even when Buffy found it impossible to express her fears and apprehensions. Although she was careful not to be over-protective, she was Buffy's protection in a hostile world. Such nurturing would prove to be invaluable for the emotionally vulnerable child.

Buffy feels that "it wasn't possible to be an Indian in my town. I lived in New England, where people didn't believe in Indians. They thought the Indians were all dead or stuffed in museums like wolves and eagles. In those small New England towns, Native Americans can feel sort of invisible as they go to school. They're just licked by the lack of reality about themselves ... I found it very difficult growing up in New England to find real live Indian people even referenced in school ... I had to wait until I was in my teens to really start visiting Indian communities."[15] There was just so little anyone seemed to know about Indians. Or was it that this was something no one wanted to talk about?

"I didn't know how to play with other kids. I didn't learn how to play and fight, laugh and insult, trade and barter. Music was about the only thing I could do. I could skate, but I couldn't do the other stuff that girls teach each other to do. So as a teenager I sort of gave up. I was hurt and disgusted by the world. I felt like a blank cheque. So I'd pray, 'If you have anything for me to do, then I'm volunteering.' Although I didn't realize it then, I was already a musician and an artist. Most little girls don't spend hours at the piano when they're three years old."[16]

Buffy's close connection with her mother was another mainstay of her childhood. "She was real intellectual, real creative, real warm, and I'm still very close to her. Although she was part Indian, she never told me Indian stories; she seldom talked about it except when she was with my aunts and uncles, and I was playing under the table. In that sense, she was an average person of her time. But what she did tell me was that I shouldn't necessarily believe everything I read in books or saw in the movies."[17]

As a professional who worked outside the home, Winifred knew what she was talking about. She told Buffy that most people— both Indian and white—were simply ignorant. She told Buffy that when she grew up she could find out for herself.

"That was just the kind of person she was," says Buffy.[18]

CHAPTER 2

SEARCH
FOR MEANING

Buffy and her friend Janice Murphy began their official education in 1946 at West Ward School, a small wooden structure that stands to this day, just up the hill from Buffy's childhood home in Wakefield. The West Ward class was small with only twelve kids. Buffy and Janice sometimes walked together to school; later, when they had to move across town to Woodville School, they would take the bus. Janice called her friend "Bevvie." The nickname "Buffy" did not emerge until high school.[19]

"I hated being indoors in school six hours a day. I learned very fast not to argue with my teachers. Certain things were best not talked about. In school they said, 'Columbus discovered America' or, 'The American Indian was ...' They said Saint-Marie was a French name, which was true, but I was not French. My teachers told me music was lines and notes and paper, a matter of decoding, a matter of coordination between the eyes and the paper. I never disagreed with them. I just learned to keep my head down and avoid conflict. Then I'd go home and play my own fake-classical music."[20]

Despite Buffy's artistic inclinations, her talent was not readily apparent to her teachers. Nor did she feel that she was that smart, especially when it came to math. "I think other kids must have thought I was odd—this kid who lives for arts that exist only in her own head. I wasn't the one in the class who was the artistic kid, although I could paint and draw at home. And I wasn't the musical kid, either. That wasn't me. And what they called music class I never understood at all and did poorly at it."[21]

Buffy could not understand what the European notation system had to do with music. Trying to decode all those little notes, lines, and spaces seemed irrelevant when all she had to do was listen and play what was in her head. Buffy thought music class shouldn't be called "music." She didn't have a clue in class and her teachers didn't perceive that she was musical.[22]

"I was being told that their reality was not what I was experiencing as my reality. I was obviously a natural musician and a natural artist and a natural dancer—like most kids—but both my Indian-ness and my artistic reality were not what the schoolbooks described. So where did that leave me? I may be wrong about it but I think all kids are full of natural talent."[23]

Although Buffy was a natural musician, she didn't consider herself to be a musician with "a capital M" because she couldn't do it the way teachers said one was supposed to do it. So, as a child, she felt different in some major ways and often didn't fit in.[24]

Buffy's third-grade teacher, Miss Marché, took Buffy's class to study American Indians and see Indian artifacts at the Museum of Natural History in nearby Boston. They did see Indians there—dead—alongside the dinosaurs. "That had a huge impact on me. Huge! I knew I existed. I wanted to exist. To see Native American people alongside the dinosaurs dead and not existing, and having my teacher and my classmates all believe that there was no such thing anymore, well that explains a few things about me!"[25]

Buffy's identity as a Native American left her feeling that she stood out even more than she already did, so she didn't talk about it much except with Leonard (Lenny) Bayrd, a member of the Narragansett Tribe and part of the only other Indian family in town. "They lived on the other side of the lake. I rode my bicycle to their house all the time. I could never get enough of being with them. I knew that's where I wanted to be."[26]

The only trace left of American Indians in Wakefield seemed to be the ubiquitous wooden Indian statues that can still be found outside some stores there. Also perplexing to Buffy were the Wakefield High School majorettes, who were outfitted in Indian costumes, complete with full feather headdresses made by Bayrd. Today, such a display would be viewed as a mockery of the region's American Indian heritage; however, at the time, Buffy admired the handicraft that went into making these beautiful headdresses. Buffy was an excellent baton twirler but membership on the squad was by vote and she was not popular enough. Fortunately, Buffy always felt welcome at Bayrd's small Indian Trading Post and spent many hours there looking at his Indian crafts, learning beadwork, and drinking in his stories.

The Narragansett have a painful history. Ninety percent of their numbers perished during King Phillip's War, an armed conflict between Native Americans and New England's English colonists in 1675, and many of the survivors were sold as slaves to the West Indies. Bayrd was a war veteran who then became the town mailman. He was Narragansett and was quiet but proud of his culture. Bayrd liked to sit outside his shop, carving. Sometimes people would drive by and shout defamations and obscenities such as "Get a job, damn lazy Indian!" Bayrd's grandson, Len Rose, remembers wanting to throw rocks at those cars, but his grandfather told him just to ignore the taunts.

The Bayrds offered Buffy another view of her identity. Lenny Bayrd was also known by his Indian name Wamblesakee (Eagle Claw). Looking for a change after twenty-seven years as a letter carrier, Bayrd had purchased an underdeveloped lot on Main Street at the head of Lake Quannapowitt and built the Indian Trading Post, a teepee-shaped craft shop, where he pursued his true passion of displaying his beautiful and authentic Native American creations. So good were his crafts and finely-beaded clothing that they came to be in great demand by Hollywood for their "cowboy and Indian" productions. His work was featured in a 1954 *Life* magazine article.[27]

The home where Bayrd lived with his wife, Ruth, was attached to the shop. Buffy recalls that Bayrd gave her her first dose of Indian reality and became something of a cornerstone of her identity. His presence and humble craft store were a revelation in a town like Wakefield, where everyone seemed to believe that American

Indians no longer existed. Buffy felt comfortable around him and sensed that she could trust him.

Bayrd loved to have children around and his house was open to them. He would tease kids, trying to scare them, and joke around with them. He was a brave man in the face of injustice. When his grandson, Len Rose, was kicked out of school for wearing what was believed to be a Nazi symbol, Bayrd protested that the whirlwind symbol was in fact used by Native Americans to signify healing. Len was exonerated. Bayrd's bravery extended to personal injury, as well. He once cut his fingers badly, his grandson remembers, and went to hospital calmly and without complaining. He was well-known but yet not really accepted as an equal by whites. When Bayrd passed into the spirit world in 1990, his work promoting Indian arts was carried on by Len Rose. Although Bayrd's collection was sold in New Mexico, Len carries on his legacy through his online Bayrd's Trading Post.[28]

Buffy's main obligation was to attend school and, despite the trials, she had some happy moments. Sometimes after school Buffy and Janice Murphy would go to the local drugstore and have root beer floats for fifteen cents. They briefly joined a Girl Scout troop but neither of the girls was able to continue paying their dues so it didn't last long. Around seventh-grade, Janice remembers Buffy inviting her to go horseback riding. Not knowing how to ride, she was afraid, but she remembers being impressed at how good a rider Buffy was. Janice was also not musically inclined but remembers Buffy as a natural who could easily play although she couldn't read music. She also remembers that Buffy enjoyed taking a school dancing class. "It was square dancing or ballroom dancing—the boys were on one side and the girls on the other." She and Buffy were so poor, each "only had one good dress," she laughs. She remembers Buffy as always being kind, "never saying a mean thing," pleasant, and a lot of fun.

However, Buffy's pleasant exterior belied a troubled inner life. As a youth, Buffy sometimes felt like her life had collapsed and folded. She reflects: "I think the most important thing that happens to a child who is abused, embarrassed, and tormented, is the child learns that the word 'no' does not work—it only makes things worse. So as an adult this kind of child grows up to be an abused spouse or girlfriend. You know, if you never dare to recognize that you are about to be hurt, you never develop that sense of seeing it coming. I never developed that sense so I was later an abused wife, an abused girlfriend. I never thought about it a lot until I was in my 30s."[29]

The frequency of any moments of joy Buffy might have shared with Janice, however, slowed to a trickle when the girls entered the imposing brick, factory-like Wakefield High School and kids started to form into cliques. Janice remembers Wakefield as a very status-conscious town. "Lily-white Wakefield I called it! Some who were friendly before wouldn't even look at you anymore." High-school society was broken up into different groups. The wealthier people from "up the hill" and their kids were called "the pack." Other groups formed along ethnic and family lines, such as the few

Puerto Ricans or the Italians. The popular kids, usually from better-off families, became the class leaders and heads of clubs.

Buffy always entered the school through the back door near the parking lot in order to avoid attention. She and Janice were outsiders who were not accepted into cliques and friendships. Worse, they slowly became alienated from one another as the result of different learning streams. The girls had chosen different courses, with Buffy following the academic stream that would lead to university, while Janice, at her parents' urging, followed the vocational stream that emphasized secretarial skills.

Because of their different programs, the two friends gradually lost contact completely. John Palumbo, Janice's husband, also knew Buffy in high school and remembers her as a pretty girl, walking down the school corridor with her arms full of books, all alone, and with the saddest, most distant look in her eyes. While Buffy felt isolated, she did try joining the choral and glee clubs to indulge in her enjoyment of music, but her heart wasn't in it.

When she left school, Janice married and had a family. She was kept so busy raising her children that she wasn't even aware of Buffy's rapid rise to stardom until she saw her old friend being interviewed on television several years later. Janice felt happy for Buffy's success and many years later they rekindled their friendship.

Buffy remembers her awkwardness in high school: "I tried to be just like all the other girls. I cut my hair short and, when they bleached their hair, I tried to bleach my hair, and I, you know, wore their lipstick and makeup, but the shades were never right for me.

"I tried to dress like them but it didn't help, and I was just a person who never fit in with the crowd and I was miserable. When I was about a junior in high school, I guess, I thought, 'I don't know what I'm going to do with my life.' I wasn't a singer at the time. I said, 'I guess I'll be a teacher,' you know, 'I guess I'd like to do that.'"[30]

Of high school, Buffy admits, "I was a lousy student in high school because they taught us a lot of bull, but I loved college." Yet growing up in Massachusetts and Maine had its advantages: "I got to know a majority of people as I may not have gotten to know them, for better or worse, in a mono-racial or mono-ethnic community. Teaching of American history was distorted and biased. Like many other students in that situation, I just kept quiet and learned what I could." Buffy's ability to see how biased and ethnocentric her education was, perhaps led her to believe that the differences between peoples can be bridged by quality education and understanding—something that has become one of her life's goals.

Fortunately, Winifred made Buffy aware of the value of good books, as she saw many in her work as an editor and avid reader. "She made me aware of the fact that books that I might come in contact with might not always tell me the truth," says Buffy. "This is what I owe her the most for. Because, if I had grown up like many Indian children do in a non-Indian city, I might have learned about Indians from the non-Indians. But instead, I was made aware by my mom, who is part Indian, that these books are not always true or accurate and that I always should be aware of the fact that things might not be as is written."[31]

As a teenager, Buffy could never escape the music she heard in her head. She dreamed of having a musical instrument, such as a guitar, that she could carry around with her. Buffy obtained her first guitar when Albert gave her money on her sixteenth birthday to purchase one from a second-hand store. However, she had no one to show her how to tune it so she had to figure out her own ways to do it. Experimenting endlessly, she would learn to tune the instrument thirty different ways.

Buffy's most treasured moments of her teenage years were summer vacations spent in the family trailer in Naples, Maine, near Sebago Lake State Park. She slept outside most nights in an army surplus jungle hammock. It was during those vacations in the pristine forest that Buffy, always the loner, began to experiment with writing her own songs to guitar accompaniment. She would take her guitar to the woods or out by the lake and explore the music in her head, developing her own distinctive and haunting sound.

Songwriting would become an increasingly important part of her personal life. "Sometimes I'd listen to the radio. Oh, Elvis Presley! I was such a fan. I'd never seen a boy like that in my town or I would have had a better time."[32] Little did Buffy imagine that one day Elvis would sing one of her songs over and over again, live and on albums. And, at this stage in her life, she would never have dreamed that the musical prowess honed in the Maine woods would one day allow her to buy and maintain a 200-year-old house in those same beloved forests.

As the end of high school approached, Buffy did not know for sure if she would be going to university so she decided to enquire at one of the country's most highly regarded music schools, Berklee School of Music in Boston. Berklee is now the world's largest independent music college and a leader in contemporary music. Buffy mustered all of her courage and took the train to Boston with high hopes. She walked in and shyly spoke with the receptionist. Buffy said that she'd like to talk to someone about enrolling, saying that she could play well but couldn't read music. The receptionist dashed Buffy's dream, responding that any applicant unable to read music would never be accepted in Berklee.[33]

Ironically, about ten years later, Buffy was invited to Berklee as a concert artist and was paid a whole lot of money. Another time she came back again to teach Berklee students about electronic music, which was very new to them but not to Buffy. Still later, Buffy was hired to teach a workshop on digital film scoring.

During the 1990s, a professor in the Berklee composition department told Buffy that she was probably musically dyslexic and that was why she was able to write for a symphony, but the next day would be unable to read it back. The professor had heard of similar cases and said there was a study being done on this type of music dyslexia, called dyscalculia, which would cause a person difficulty in areas involving logic or math but was not a problem in other areas, such as philosophy. Buffy had always had to learn to do what she wanted to do in a different way—using her strengths. With her music dyslexia, Buffy states that she tends to have a "helicopter view" of things, for example, being able "to see" the whole song as one whole piece instead of from measure to measure. Since Buffy first learned about her condition, a lot of material has been published about it.

Throughout her career, and to this day, Buffy could not read music. In a 2005 interview she said, "I'm musically illiterate. I'm kind of musically dyslexic. I cannot read notes but I can write out a chart while the music is still in my head ... I rely on memory and what's inside."[34]

Her condition has caused her a great deal of consternation: "I've often felt uncomfortable with other musicians. I always felt as though I was under-qualified. When it came to playing music with a bunch of guys, especially sidemen, when I was making more money than they were, and they [found] out I [couldn't] read and stuff, oh, man, they would be hard on me. They would give me the business, say little humiliating things; it kind of broke my heart sometimes."[35]

After finishing the twelfth grade and with Berklee no longer an option, Buffy decided to explore the option of going to university. By this time her older brother had joined the Air Force and her younger sister was then ten years old. Buffy was anxious to escape the threatening familiarity of home. When Buffy left for university in 1959, it opened up an exciting new world that left her with little desire to return to Wakefield, though she remained close to Winifred and some of her other relatives.

CHAPTER 3

JOURNEY OF
SELF-DISCOVERY

Buffy Sainte-Marie entered the University of Massachusetts at Amherst in the fall of 1959, as an eighteen-year-old freshman. At the time, UMass was a state college of about 5,000 students located 145 km (90 mi.) northwest of Boston.[36]

Winifred had found Buffy a government loan for students planning to go into teaching—she was accepted only two weeks before classes began. Buffy was unsure about university, but Winifred advised her to give it a try, saying, "If it doesn't work out then come back." Buffy was the first in her family to attend university. Her early grades were mainly Bs and Cs with the occasional A and D thrown in, but these marks steadily improved as she progressed through her degree program.[37]

Initially, Buffy contemplated becoming a veterinarian in addition to focusing on teaching. Mass Aggie, as the university had affectionately been nicknamed years before, was a very good agricultural college. Buffy took biology, botany, geology, astronomy, and zoology, but quickly realized that a veterinarian needs to be a scientist—math and chemistry were both weak subjects for her (likely due to the dyscalculia she would learn about much later). By sophomore year, Buffy realized that, although she loved animals and science, without chemistry she would never become an animal doctor and changed her program.

Many years later, Buffy took consolation in the knowledge that real world veterinarians needed more than chemistry to succeed— they also require a strict objectivity that allows them to handle injured and sick animals, as well as dealing with pet owners. Today Buffy laughs and says she is more of a pet lover than a scientist and always will be.

The University of Massachusetts offered classes on world religions, a field in which Buffy had a keen interest. She signed up for an introduction to philosophy course taught by Dr. Clarence Shute and discovered that people all over the world have unique, personal, and varied ways of relating to the Creator. She was impressed by Dr. Shute and he became her mentor as she took other courses in world religions, eventually focusing on those of Asia.

Buffy pursued a major reflecting her primary interest in Asian philosophy and later added the requirements for a teaching degree. Buffy remembers teaching in a first-grade classroom prior to graduation. She kept a rabbit in the classroom for her young pupils to interact with and, during holidays when the rabbit had nowhere else to stay, Buffy would sneak him into her dorm.

Buffy was the first student to pursue a degree in Asian philosophy at UMass but the university did not offer enough classes or credits to award a degree. Fortunately, a new intercollegiate program enabled students to earn additional credits from classes at three other local institutions, all of which were excellent colleges. Buffy rode a bus to take classes in Buddhism and Hinduism at Smith College; had seminars with Jesuit scholars and Bible studies at Mt. Holyoke; and took additional courses at Amherst College.[38] She even found time to act in an Amherst production of Arthur Miller's *The Crucible.*

Buffy found the college experience fascinating and inspiring. She loved both her majors and feels to this day that university helped save her life: "Being an Oriental philosophy major brought me in touch with the international community. I hung around with people from Africa and India and all over the world, and we'd go out to have something to eat together, and we'd talk about things that maybe the girl in the dorm room next to me would never be interested in.

"I really feel as though I owe the University of Massachusetts everything, in supporting my sense of curiosity and wanting to know, and I feel as though college is the best thing that can happen to a person in that it gives you four years, if you can hang in there, of having a roof over your head, something to eat, being away from your family; it's like a safe place to explore whatever you want to put in your head."[39]

It was through university courses that Buffy began to discover how the history of American Indians unfolded. Buffy's friend, Patricia Woods, whom she'd known at UMass, recalls how elated Buffy was after taking a history class that addressed American

Indian issues. "It was like a light bulb which went off in her!" Buffy was able to delve into the true story of the American Indian by reading works like John Collier's *Indians of the Americas* and Jack Forbes's *The Indian in America's Past*. These texts confirmed what Winifred had told her as a child. "I was always glad that my mother had prepared me that way ... that the Indians did not lose to the white people because of fair fights and majority odds and superior weaponry, but that the Indians have been cheated and cheated and cheated again and still are cheated and cheated again."[40]

Buffy was learning to see Indigenous peoples through the unique lens of an abused child. She knew that, when someone is persecuted over time, they will eventually lose self-confidence and self-respect. Buffy, as a performer, was able to put her collected knowledge to good use, describing her youthful experiences to audiences in rallying speeches like the following, made in 1966:

"American people act as though Indians lost because of superior odds and superior weaponry and fair fights. But that's not the way it happened! It's about time we started to raise a generation of kids who realize that nations, like individuals, make mistakes, and that mistakes must be corrected if proper and straight growth is ever to be resumed ... There are reasons why Indians are in the worst state of poverty of any minority in North America. It's not because we're stupid, not because we're slobs—it's because we've been mistreated!"[41]

Buffy's university friends and mentors helped her find the courage to begin performing. Buffy roomed in the French wing of the Abigail Adams House, where she would regularly sing her songs for other girls in the dorm. One of the housemothers, Teresa de Kerpely, the British widow of the famous Hungarian cellist, also noticed Buffy's burgeoning talent. De Kerpely played Edith Piaf records and encouraged Buffy to explore her passion in songs. She emphasized the idea of songwriting as a meaningful occupation instead of a hobby. That de Kerpely also spoke French, a language for which Buffy had a special affinity, was another advantage.

Buffy's dad felt that if you wanted to become a singer, you should emulate the pop/Las Vegas sound of Connie Francis in order to become successful. But Buffy had an eclectic affinity for the music of Elvis Presley, Little Richard, and other rock n' roll singers. She was inspired by Miles Davis and the singing and dancing of Spanish flamenco artist Carmen Amaya. Nineteen-sixty-two witnessed the burgeoning folk music movement on American campuses, and this was when Buffy made her first real inroads into singing in public. She continued to compose original songs, as she had done since she was small, drawing from her own experiences, insights, and curiosity. She sang her songs for fellow students and found they were well received.

At UMass, Buffy met another singer who would become a lifelong friend—the multifaceted, contemporary blues musician and singer-songwriter Taj Mahal (Henry Fredericks). Mahal discovered his new name in a dream. Son of an American mother whose heritage was a Creole blend of Black and Native American, and a father from the Caribbean, Mahal was a year younger than Buffy. He began studies in agriculture and moved into animal sciences before finding that he had significant allergies in any agricultural setting. Mahal remembers first reading about Buffy in the local paper. An advertisement for the *Springfield Union* noted that "Miss Beverly J. St. Marie is going to be singing at the Coffee House. She is a student at the University of Massachusetts and a Native American."

Mahal first met Buffy in 1961 because he was interested in speaking with someone who wrote and sang her own creations. He was impressed. UMass had a music room with three pianos and five or six listening centres. Patricia Woods remembers that Mahal would arrange to have the auditorium opened early so he could practise with his band. Many student musicians hung out there, including Buffy, and one day they met. The two musicians sat down in a stairwell that was a natural echo chamber and played a couple of songs together on their acoustic guitars. From that point on Mahal became Buffy's fan.[42] It was entirely mutual.

Buffy's original lyrics and passionate feelings addressed wide-ranging social concerns. Although she was tiny in stature at only 5 feet, 2 inches (1.6 m), Buffy's long hair and bold look, combined with her strong voice and the directness of her message, gave her a huge presence.

Buffy recalls this exciting time on the cusp of her career. She began singing at a coffee house called the Saladin, located just off campus in an old Victorian house with dark mahogany walls. Upon entering the foyer, guests found a room to the left with small tables, each with a lamp—basically a big room on the main floor of a tenant house where large numbers of students, up to seventy, would hang out. Coffee was the strongest beverage served. Buffy often appeared in unusual outfits, sometimes with a burlap poncho or wearing gold lipstick. She sang her own songs: some were love songs, others were about social issues, and some were country songs readily adapted to guitar.

"I always think the music is in the instrument. When I go to choose a guitar, I always can tell the ones that are going to have a lot of songs in them. I know that sounds silly but something about the instrument brings about certain kinds of songs and certain tunings, too. It's the same thing with keyboards. They bring about a certain kind of song, from me, anyway.

"So from the very beginning I was just like when I was a little kid, I was writing happy, sad, weird, regular, all different kinds of combinations, and at the Saladin coffee house, too, I'd sing some songs that had a message. The type of song that ... "Universal Soldier," or "Now That the Buffalo's Gone" would fall into, too. I was writing love songs, "Until It's Time for You to Go"-type pop songs, songs in weird tunings, rockabilly—anything I felt like."[43]

Buffy did not have titles for all of her songs back then. Her lyrics explored love and war and protest, and all were played from memory. In addition to her own compositions, Buffy often sang folk favourites that drew a sizeable audience. Her repertoire ranged from the Bible-based "Ananias" to the fiery "Now That the Buffalo's Gone." Another song, "Mayoo Sto Hoon," sung in Hindi, reflected her interest in Asian philosophy. Although Buffy was paid a modest $5 per night, Taj Mahal felt she had a great fan base because she never held anything back when she played. Buffy's performance was always a straight shot.

Oh it's written in books and in song
That we've been mistreated and wronged
Well over and over I hear those same words
From you good lady and you good man
Well listen to me if you care where we stand
And you feel you're a part of these ones
"Now That the Buffalo's Gone"

Buffy was a serious student and her awareness and curiosity blossomed at many levels. "Junior and senior year I was in a dorm studying very hard. I had a double major, Oriental philosophy and teaching. I didn't think I was ever going to be a professional singer. I thought I would probably have some kind of a job with religion and the arts in India. That's what I expected to do. Either that or teach on a reservation."[44]

It was not until the summer after her senior year in college that she shifted her energies and focus to the world of folk music. "My only goal in my music life was to write songs that would be meaningful in all kinds of different countries in all kinds of different generations. That was kind of what inspired me.

"As a college student just writing songs, I had a great model in the true folk songs that have lasted hundreds of years and that cross language barriers. Like an antique chair that generation after generation cares for, some songs will last for generations. That's what I always enjoyed trying for if the subject was important—to create these songs about the human condition well enough that they would make sense all over the world in more than one generation. I'm really glad to see that people still find a song useful and appreciated."[45]

During her last year at university, Buffy learned there was an opening for a female singer at an obscure watering hole called the Melody Bar in the nearby town of Springfield, Massachusetts. She was hired in 1961 by the bar's regular entertainer, Paul Corbin, a kind family man of strong Catholic conviction. Both Buffy and Corbin were easygoing and the music was fun. Buffy played a few originals but also included pop and jazz tunes recorded by Julie London, Joni James, and the Everly Brothers. Gigs at the Melody Bar often ran late, so Buffy secured permission from the university's Dean of Girls to stay in Springfield with the Corbin family, which included Corbin's wife, Julie, and their six children. Buffy was very attached to the Corbins during the time she stayed with them. Their son, Peter, who was twelve at the time, was a great friend.

At the bar, Corbin would play piano and Buffy would play guitar, singing separately or duets on songs such as "Bye Bye Blackbird." Sometimes she would play concert sets at Springfield's Old Candy Factory, which featured such professional acts as the Grandison Singers, a gospel group she loved. These experiences provided Buffy with an invaluable taste of what a career in singing was all about, and they helped her develop the type of polish that would later pay off. She relished these early audiences because they provided her with an unparalleled opportunity to express her views. Buffy also overcame stage fright by concentrating on the song instead of on herself.

Although Buffy was learning the fundamentals of performing as a singer, she remained seriously in love with her studies. Buffy wanted to complete university and was thinking about travelling to India to study religion and art at a school founded by Mahatma Gandhi and renowned poet Rabindranath Tagore, two of modern India's greatest thinkers. Alternatively, she considered finding a job teaching at an elementary school on an American Indian reservation.

Buffy did her practice teaching in Greenfield, Massachusetts, where she thought a lot about parents using school as a babysitter without concern for what their children were learning. Remembering her own grade school years, where her musical talent was not recognized because of her inability to decode Europe's system of written notation, Buffy could see a clear need for improvements in education. She also felt that teaching on a reservation would no doubt tie her hands and sew up her mouth. Her song, "Suffer the Little Children" expresses a scathing view of the education system:

School bell go ding dong ding
The children all line up
They do what they are told
Take a little drink from the liar's cup

Buffy realized the United States Bureau of Indian Affairs was set up to make business deals destined to annihilate Indian cultures under the guise of assimilation. It seemed to her that the American government wanted Indians to disappear. She was appalled at the way governments broke Indian treaties and recognized simple greed as the obvious motive to confiscate Indian lands. Buffy did not want to teach lies to schoolchildren. She felt she would not be able to tolerate that kind of potential employer.[46]

Universities in the 1960s were often left wing with a politically aggressive student body. Buffy was not so bold, preferring to take a gentle but firm stand. Former Minister of Education for Saskatchewan, Keith Goulet, a Métis fluent in Cree, remembers the conformity of the early 1960s and lack of questioning of society. In those days you were supposed to keep quiet about racism and just say "yes sir, no sir" to everything.

Buffy expected to graduate with honours from the University of Massachusetts in the spring of 1962, with a degree in Asian philosophy with a minor in teaching. She was surprised to be voted one of the ten most outstanding graduating seniors in her class. However, she was crushed to discover she would not be allowed to graduate with her class. Speech class was a basic requirement for all sophomore students and if a student did well enough on his or her initial speech, they were exempted from the course. Buffy's speech was excellent and she was released from the requirement. The university had a record of Buffy's exemption, but failed to inform her or her advisor that she would need to make up the credit for the exempted course. When it came time to graduate, Buffy was not allowed to walk across the stage with her classmates to receive her scroll. Patricia Woods recalls the irony: Buffy was prevented from graduating with her colleagues because she lacked a half-credit speech class requirement from which she had been exempted by excellence, yet, a few months later, she was making impassioned speeches to huge crowds. Buffy's official diploma was not released until years later, after the misunderstanding had been cleared up.

After missing the graduation ceremony, Buffy did two things: she went to New York with her guitar to check out the coffee house scene, and set out to explore Native American communities. Buffy had already amassed substantial singing experience in Massachusetts coffee houses and found that even her modest earnings were enough to fund further explorations of Native North American culture. Both experiences made a lasting impact on what Buffy would choose to do with the rest of her life.

Buffy visited Akwesasne Reserve on the New York–Canada border in 1962 and made friends at the Six Nations Reserve in Ontario. She spent time as a member of the National Indian Youth Council and was on Sargent Shriver's Upward Bound committee in Washington, D.C. during the 1960s. Buffy also spent time with relocated Indian people in Toronto and hung around the Native Friendship Centre on Spadina Avenue. Little by little, she explored and grasped contemporary Indian life both in Canada and in the United States.

In the early 1960s, First Nations communities on Manitoulin Island in Ontario were among the earliest to revive powwows, inviting dancers from the prairies who still retained the pure forms of the powwow celebration to share their knowledge. It was during a 1962 visit to the Wikwemikong powwow on Manitoulin Island that Buffy first came into contact with her possible relatives.

Buffy took the train to Wikwemikong to meet and spend time with Rosemary Fisher, Wilf Pelletier, and others of their extended family. At the powwow, Buffy was introduced to Emile Piapot, a Cree travelling with several other singers and dancers from Saskatchewan's Piapot Reserve. Emile spoke both Cree and English and Buffy explained that she had been told that she had been born to an Indian family in Saskatchewan.

There was an easy rapport between them. Emile quietly listened to Buffy, then shared how he had once given up an infant daughter. Perhaps he sensed something familiar about the way Buffy looked and behaved. Buffy was thrilled when Emile invited her to visit his family in Saskatchewan.

Emile Piapot was reputed to be the last living son of Chief Piapot, leader of a band of Plains Cree who were known to be proud hunters, traders, and warriors whose ancestors had migrated to the plains of what is now Canada. He was one of those remarkable and versatile leaders capable of seeing his people through extremely challenging times. Chief Piapot was more than a political leader and diplomat who was wise enough to understand the importance of signing Treaty Number Four with the British Crown in 1874; he

Buffy (centre) with Emile Piapot and Clara Starblanket Piapot

was also a spiritual person and accomplished warrior who fought peacefully to see that the changes would truly bring benefits to his people.

Emile Piapot returned home from the Ontario powwow very excited. He told his wife, Clara, of his encounter with Buffy and that he had invited her to Saskatchewan to visit. Later that fall, Buffy arrived at the Regina airport and called the Piapot band office, which relayed the message of her arrival to Emile.

There were no home phones on the reserve so Buffy could not call Emile directly to say, "My plane has arrived." Similarly, the Piapot family did not know exactly what Buffy's arrival time was, so no one was at the airport to meet her. Buffy hailed a taxi and told the driver to take her to the Piapot Reserve. The cabbie did not know the way. When the taxi finally made it to the reserve, it promptly became stuck in the snow. People on the reserve came and dug the cab out. Buffy's niece, Debbie, remembers the first time she saw her aunt: a tiny woman who wore a white straw hat and talked a lot. Debbie found her captivating.

Emile's house, with its peeling maroon and white paint, was located in a sparsely populated village behind the band office, set a little back from the road and hidden by maple trees you had to circumvent to reach the front of the house. The house was not fancy. There was a dirt floor and a wood stove. Over the next many years, Clara showed Buffy how to crush chokecherries with rocks and make pemmican. Buffy listened to Emile sing with a hand drum. It was frigid when they went to sleep.

Brenda Star was only twelve when Buffy first arrived at the Piapot home. She had also been adopted into the Piapot family. A common Cree tradition provides that, if a family has lost one child, eventually their hearts will bring another child into the family by adoption.

One day after school, Buffy said to Brenda, "Let's go for a walk," and the two wandered along a coulee, up a big ravine. Buffy was in exploring mode. Back at the house, she asked Emile, "Where can we find a good chokecherry tree?" Emile directed her to a clump of trees partway up a nearby hill. When Buffy found them and asked Brenda if she knew what a mouthbow was, Brenda did not know.

Buffy described the mouthbow as probably the oldest musical instrument in the world. It is basically a hunting weapon on which, Buffy believes, someone figured out how to make music. Brenda later recognized the mouthbow in a December 1965 *Life Magazine* article on Buffy as the very same one that Buffy had fashioned from that chokecherry tree.[47]

Emile was a powerful medicine man with a marked gift for healing. People travelled from all over the province to consult him. Brenda remembers one time Emile was called to the Dundurn area near Saskatoon. A young girl in a wheelchair was brought to see Emile, who was seeing his patients in a large healing tent. Brenda hung around outside listening to drumming and singing. "All of a sudden, everything went silent," she recalls. Brenda sneaked around the front and peered through the flap. She could see the patient lying on a bed. Suddenly, the girl sat up! She heard Emile ask the girl, "Are you all right?" before telling her, "Get up from the bed!" The girl rose and began to walk around. Emile used to tell Brenda about how his father, Chief Piapot, also known as Flash-in-the-Sky Boy, had also been a powerful leader and medicine person.[48]

Emile would stand up for what he believed when needed. Sometimes band officials tried to hold private meetings at the band office. Emile would show up and, when told the event was private, would say, "No, I have a right. It's a public meeting. If you don't want me here, you will have to haul me out!" Emile never let anybody "talk smart" to him. Brenda says that Buffy demonstrates similar qualities.

Emile and Buffy spent a lot of time together, just appreciating the gifts of the Creator. They spent hours talking about the old ways and burning sweet grass. Buffy was not well-known in Saskatchewan and those early days at the Piapots's home were a welcome respite.

Buffy spent a lot of time with Emile and Clara and became comfortable with life on the reserve. She met everyone in the family: Clara and Emile's son, Alvin, and his wife, Marie; Ronnie, whose wife was Violet; and daughter, Cora, who married Joe Obey. She recalls with a great deal of warmth and appreciation how well the family treated her and felt she could never spend enough time with them. Unfortunately, a search of birth records revealed nothing.

Buffy remained with Emile and his family for a few weeks during that first memorable visit. She returned to the United States on an emotional high, feeling that she had now found support for her feelings of identity.

During a subsequent visit to the Piapot family, the powwow announcer called her name and invited her family to join her. Buffy was overwhelmed and humbled as the singers voiced an honour song, formally adopting her into the Piapot family. This gave her a new inspiration, and Buffy discovered an environment where she could live quietly and without fear.

Part of a formal family acceptance meant that Buffy was given a Cree name. Emile escorted her to the house of another respected elder, J.B. Kaiswatum. He became her nikwemes, her name-giver. From him, Buffy received the name Medicine Bird Singing. Cree name-giving is a solemn process, and the names are treated with utmost respect, seldom used outside of the family. Much later, in 1976, Buffy was also given the name Star Woman by Elder Ed Calf Robe of the Blackfoot Siksika Nation at the memorial for activist Nelson Small Legs, Jr.[49]

Buffy was very grateful to be able to learn of the "way of the sweet grass" from Emile and the other elders. She was privileged to know many of the spiritual leaders involved in the rain dance: Emile Piapot, Henry Ironchild, John Rockthunder, Pius Kaiswatum, J.B. Kaiswatum, George Obey, and Marius Nahnepowitz. Buffy never had the sense of learning lessons; instead, just by spending so much time with these special people, she absorbed culture and traditional information and picked up much of the Cree language as she watched and listened. Buffy was particularly impressed by the tenderness and love she saw demonstrated among all she met.

Buffy kept in close contact with her adoptive Cree family. In

Buffy chats with Pius Kaiswatum on the Piapot Reserve.

the late 1960s, Buffy brought her part-Native Hawaiian husband, Dewain Bugbee, out to the reserve, and stayed three weeks with the family in the tiny two-bedroom house. Emile and Clara had one bedroom while Brenda was relegated to the living-room sofa. It was winter and Bugbee could not believe how cold it got. Everyone was covered with thick blankets and they could see the mist from their breath.

The hospitality was always heart-warming. Every morning,

Emile could be heard burning sweet grass and singing. Then he would shout in Cree to Brenda to get up and get the stove fire going. After a while, the wood stove would be roaring, producing cozy warmth, and the comforting smell of bacon and bannock would fill the kitchen.

Buffy was excited about taking Bugbee on a tour of Saskatchewan's Qu'Appelle Valley. Later in the visit, Clara took Buffy aside before she left and whispered in her ear, "Buffy, I want a grandchild before I pass on."

"I'll see what I can do," Buffy replied, giggling.

"I have always been so grateful for what people who are older than me have taught me," says Buffy. "Kokum and Mushum [Clara and Emile] and others accepted me as a peer and a relative."[50] Clara had diabetes and passed to the spirit side in 1981, with Buffy at her bedside. She mourned at Emile's funeral a decade later.

Meanwhile, in faraway New York City, Buffy's singing career was beginning to rapidly unfold.

CHAPTER 4

THE
GREENWICH VILLAGE
SCENE

Greenwich Village, a neighbourhood of narrow, oddly-oriented streets on the west side of Manhattan, began as a Dutch settlement in the 1630s. Before that, the area was called *Sapokanikan* or "tobacco field" by its original Lenape Native American inhabitants. The area, with its low rents and good location (not too far south from the skyscrapers of Manhattan), soon became a magnet for American counterculture poets and painters. The Village became famous when a handful of writers, including Jack Kerouac and Allen Ginsberg, began to speak out against what they perceived as an unhealthy conformity in American society. They spawned the 1950s Beat Generation, with its emphasis on creative experience, intellectual critique, and free expression. By the early 1960s, another creative explosion developed: singer-songwriters dedicated to writing their own songs with their own unique messages. Peter La Farge, Bob Dylan, Phil Ochs, Eric Anderson, and others passionately addressed social issues. Nobody had even heard of hippies yet.

In the summer of 1963, having explored her cultural roots, Buffy headed to Greenwich Village. She ventured to MacDougall and Bleeker streets between West Third and Fourth—a mecca for aspiring folk singers. "I just took my guitar and a head full of songs to New York and people loved them."[51] Buffy's striking appearance, original songs, and unique voice brought her quick recognition in such venues as The Gaslight Cafe, Gerde's Folk City, and the Bitter End. However, the folk music scene would prove to be challenging. As Suze Rotolo, then Bob Dylan's girlfriend, noted, "The folk music world was primarily a boy's club. Girls knew their place if they were girlfriends. Even if they were folksingers working their way up just like the guys, their position was not quite the same."[52]

Buffy's first New York gig was at Gerde's Folk City, where many newcomers began their career by singing at an open microphone. Bob Dylan was in the audience, loved what he saw, and advised Buffy to "go on down the street and see Sam at the Gaslight,"[53] referring to Sam Hood, manager of The Gaslight Cafe. There, she sang at another open-mike event and ended up with a bit of money once the hat was passed around. Buffy learned to live cheaply, staying at the YWCA and frequently dining on beans smothered with copious amounts of ketchup and mustard.

Reminiscing about that time in her life, Buffy acknowledges that she was dressed wrong for the coffee house scene. While other girls were wearing granny dresses, Buffy wore fancy outfits from the Frederick's catalogue (with hems cut into zigzags) and high spiked heels.

Buffy's previous trips to New York had allowed her to see Allan Freed's live rock 'n' roll shows, featuring Little Richard, the Everly Brothers, Chuck Berry, Jerry Lee Lewis, Little Anthony and the Imperials, the Platters, Laverne Baker, and JoAnn Campbell (who impressed Buffy by coming onstage in a sparkly gown with a long train). Buffy loved the visual impact of these shows and was one of very few "folk singers" who reflected a real show business glamour, which has continued throughout her career.

The Gaslight Cafe originated as a humble, intimate, basement-cellar venue; its floor had been lowered to allow enough headspace for people to stand up. Twin stairways on either side of an upstairs stairwell led to the basement. The asymmetry of these stairways—six steps on one side and nine on the other—provided a fine prelude for improvisation. The Gaslight's capacity was 110 and it attracted the coffee crowd: people interested in hearing what poets and songwriters had to say.[54] The cafe had old round oak tables, most of which held cheap Tiffany lamps. The menu featured an impressive range of coffees, including spiced coffee, Viennese coffee, espresso Romano, and coffee Romano (frosted), all at about seventy cents a cup. Patrons could choose a Holland ham sandwich for a buck fifty, and date-nut bread for dessert.

Coffee houses were tenuous business ventures at best, because they were non-alcoholic establishments. Most entertainment clubs made their profits on the sale of liquor. At coffee houses, some patrons would nurse a lone cup of coffee for hours. Dave Van Ronk, a popular fixture in the Village and a regular at the Gaslight, said "They had the worst coffee I have ever encountered."[55]

The Gaslight was not an ideal venue. Things sometimes became so noisy that the older Italian occupants of the top-floor apartments in the three-storey structure would complain. Folk music patrons often snapped their fingers in applause rather than risk a police raid. The air conditioners were old and would break, dripping water over the area where performers stood. Despite the inconveniences; however, the Gaslight became the epicentre of the folk music explosion.

Up the street and around the corner from the Gaslight, the Bitter End was a larger, street-level venue with a bigger stage. Bill Cosby often appeared there in the early 1960s, straddling a stool in front of the brick wall at the back of the café. Cosby thought Buffy was unique. He felt that, in the light of European conquest of the Americas, it was extremely difficult for people to keep true to their own cultures, not only in their heads but also in their hearts. Buffy was someone who knew where she came from and didn't forget it. Buffy and Cosby became mutual fans. Dick Gregory, Woody Allen, and Flip Wilson also practised their routines on the Bitter End's audience.

One of Buffy's earliest acquaintances was Peter La Farge, the son of anthropologist and Pulitzer Prize-winning writer Oliver La Farge. He was rumoured to have Narragansett blood and to have spent time among the Tewa tribe in New Mexico. La Farge served in the U.S. Navy during the Korean War, earning five battle stars, but he came to criticize the war as a tragic waste of lives. La Farge spent time with young Bob Dylan, as well as Ramblin' Jack Elliot, Dave Van Ronk, and political minstrel Pete Seeger. Suze Rotolo remembered him as one of the "cowboys in the village ... with more of a tough guy presence than the others." La Farge had given Dylan a bullwhip as a present and showed him how to crack and snap it properly.[56] His songs about the Native American delivered a powerful message about injustice. For example, "The Ballad of Ira Hayes," about the Pima Indian war hero who helped raise the American flag at Iwo Jima, caught the attention of Johnny Cash, who made it into a major hit. Some music historians credit La Farge as being instrumental in initiating the Greenwich Village folk scene. Unfortunately, his premature death in 1965 at the age of thirty-three, apparently of a stroke, snuffed out what promised to be a brilliant career.

Just before his death, La Farge wrote an article for *Sing Out!* magazine in which he described Buffy as a very shy and gentle, yet complex, young Indian girl who had a wealth of compassion for the world and its people. He saw her as very private, resisting any relationship that might capture or curtail her in any way. He concluded that Buffy was a powerful, fragile, pretty, and magnificent folk queen who had more going for her than anyone else in the art.

Buffy debuted as a folk poet with a spontaneous ability to instill truth into simplicity, especially political and cultural truths. Buffy never forgot the Indian people, and her Native American message was an integral part of her psyche. During her life, Buffy turned her childhood feelings of inferiority into pride, and this became her strength as a performer. Buffy was demanding of her audiences and did not suffer fools gladly. Eric Anderson, who would later be contracted to the same recording studio as Buffy (Vanguard Records), remembers her early singing style as powerful and her message arresting, but he also knew that in order to keep the audience, she could be gentle as well.[57]

Buffy's friend, Patricia Woods, worked near Greenwich Village and witnessed first-hand Buffy's earliest years in New York City. Woods would offer Buffy her apartment as a place to stay during her weekend trips from Springfield, Mass., where she also sang in local clubs. Later, Buffy and Woods shared a place in the West Village: a walk-up apartment with two trundle beds and a tiny fire escape where Buffy liked to sit, strumming her guitar and practising her songs.

Woods recalls this post-McCarthyism period, when people were tired of suppressing their views about the social and racial injustices around them. She also remembers the excitement and buzz around Greenwich Village, with its off-Broadway experimental theatre, music, and poetry. Woods thought that Buffy was brave, although she worried about her friend's vulnerability. In the racially charged days of the civil rights movement, she knew that bad things could happen to solitary minority individuals who dissented too loudly.

Woods also recalls occasionally seeing Bob Dylan. During the early 1960s, he lived in Greenwich Village, writing his iconic

"The Times They Are a-Changin'" there. Peter La Farge lived in an apartment across the street so Buffy did not feel out of place at all. When she walked down the streets of Greenwich Village, she relished her feeling of relaxed playfulness, like the excitement before a high-school football game. Buffy believed that her contemporaries were able to make their presence known all over the streets. There was an additional sense that those in power were in trouble and worried, because students had discovered how to use their brains.[58]

Some weeks after Buffy's arrival in New York, prominent *New York Times* music critic Robert Shelton visited the Gaslight and took in her performance. He gave her an enthusiastic review: "Music Taking on New Color: An Indian Girl Sings her Compositions and Folk Songs."

"Brightening the scene is a young Algonquin girl," the review read, calling Buffy "an Indian from Sebago Lake who is making her debut at the Gaslight … Her own compositions and her vibrant way of interpreting them make Miss Sainte-Marie, at 21, one of the most promising new talents on the folk scene. Two of her songs, 'The Universal Soldier' and 'Cod'ine,' a haunting paean about narcotics addiction, are impressive musically as well as for revealing the world-awareness of the writer."[59] The Gaslight had a big copy of the review made and plastered it up in front of the café. Things were beginning to happen for Buffy. The next time Shelton came to see Buffy perform, he brought along Vanguard Records founder Maynard Solomon.

Vanguard Records was established by brothers Maynard and Seymour Solomon in New York in 1950. Initially publishers of classical music and jazz, they began experimenting with fringe music in the mid-1950s, signing the Weavers, as well as folk artists Joan Baez, Hedy West, Country Joe and the Fish, Ian and Sylvia, and Mimi and Richard Farina.[60] At the Gaslight, Maynard heard Buffy sing "It's My Way" and "Now That the Buffalo's Gone" and, despite having a reputation for being conservative in his musical tastes (he later wrote a book on Beethoven), he took a liking to her style and asked her to sign with Vanguard.

The enthusiastic reception Buffy received in Greenwich Village and the offer from Solomon to sign with Vanguard was a lot to digest. Blue Note Records, a jazz label, had also expressed interest in Buffy, which surprised her but proved an acknowledgement of her versatility.

Buffy still planned to leave for India soon to further her studies. In the fall of 1963, she returned to Maine to mull over her options. As a self-taught musician, was she really good enough to become a professional? Finally, Buffy decided she wanted to pursue a singing career and returned to New York to sign a seven-year contract with Vanguard. She believed there was a place for her songs and that, in the optimism of the times, she was in the right position and place to deliver her special message. Her first manager was Herbert Gart.

Buffy burst onto the national consciousness in 1964. Her debut album, *It's My Way*, included "Universal Soldier." Song topics ranged from incest to drug addiction. Several offerings were college-day staples.[61] Unlike many traditional folk songs of that time, Buffy's songs were largely her own material. "Universal Soldier," written as the Vietnam War escalated, would become her first big hit.[62] *All Music Guide* called it one of the most scathing topical folk albums ever made.

> *He's 5 foot 2 and he's 6 feet 4*
> *He fights with missiles and with spears*
> *He's all of 31 and he's only 17.*
> *He's been a soldier for a thousand years.*
> *He's a Catholic, a Hindu, an atheist, a Jain*
> *A Buddhist, and a Baptist and a Jew.*
> *And he knows he shouldn't kill*
> *And he knows he always will*
> *kill you for me my friend, and me for you.*
> *"Universal Soldier"*

In 1964, *Billboard* named Buffy its Best New Artist of the Year. However, she was not pursuing her folk music career for glory but because she believed she could be an instrument of change. Buffy once confided to Paul Sexton of *Billboard* that the only reason she ever became a singer in the first place was because she felt that she had something to say. "The early sixties ... things were very innocent. And it wasn't about folk music really. That's how everybody marketed it. It was really about students. It was really a free speech movement.

There was everything going on. Coming out of the beatnik era, you know, everybody was writing poetry ... poetry about not sending us to war or poetry about loving somebody or whatever ...

"So I came in at a time when there was really a very broad acceptance and tolerance for one another ... It was before the marketers got a hold of it; it was happening in coffeehouses everywhere. Coffee was the 'drug.' It wasn't alcohol. You didn't see people drinking much. I didn't see many drugs around."[63]

Not all of her experiences within the folk scene were so pristine. Buffy recalls one strange and frightening experience she had in Florida in 1963, before signing with Vanguard. She had been on the coffee house circuit for about six months and her name was getting around quickly. "While I was [in Florida] I had developed a cough and got bronchitis. It was bugging me, so I went to a doctor. He gave me some medicine for it and said, 'Yeah, you'll have to come back.' So I'd go back and he'd give me a shot. Then he'd give me some medicine and he had me get a prescription. I was held over and didn't have anywhere else to go, so this went on for a few weeks.

"Finally, I got in a car with two friends to go to Atlanta, Georgia ... Oh, man, I started getting sick! I didn't know what was wrong with me! So I had a prescription and I said, 'Well, you know, I'm probably getting sick again. I'm having a relapse.' So I went to this pharmacist in Atlanta. He said, 'How long have you been taking this?' Then he told me, 'You're in withdrawal!' I said, 'What?' This doctor, who I'm told was later arrested and jailed, was addicting me to something I never, ever would have gotten involved with.

"So my big drug experience with opiates isn't the same as that of somebody who chooses to get involved and get high with their friends. It wasn't the same at all. It was predatory. But I do know what withdrawal is about because I have been through it."[64]

Buffy later heard that this doctor had been addicting pretty young women to prescription drugs in order to turn them out as prostitutes. She suspected that, because she was by herself, just a lone girl, she would have been the perfect victim. Her angry response prompted her song "Cod'ine" about opiate addiction.

And my belly is craving, I got a shakin' in my head
Feel like I'm dyin' and I wish I was dead
If I live till tomorrow that'll be a long time
But I'll reel and I'll fall and I'll rise on cod'ine
And its real, and its real, one more time
You'll forget you're a woman, you'll forget about men
Try it just once, and you'll try it again
You'll forget about life, you'll forget about time
And you'll live off your days as a slave to cod'ine.[65]
"Cod'ine"

In 1963, legendary blues singer Janis Joplin instantly recognized the power of "Cod'ine," covered it, and made it a hit. Later, Quick Silver Messenger Service and Courtney Love would also record it. For Buffy, however, the song marked her rather unusual brush with addiction.

Although Buffy's songs were being covered by prominent musicians of the time, she seldom collaborated with others. Usually she recorded only her own work, although occasionally she would perform or record other people's songs, especially those of unknown songwriters. One friend, Patrick Sky, introduced Buffy to the mouthbow. Vanguard owner Maynard Solomon heard Sky's work and offered him a contract. Sky was one of many singers Buffy would help along the way. His 1965 debut album included several original tunes, including "Many a Mile." Buffy later covered the tune and named her second album for it.

Buffy introduced Dave Van Ronk to Patrick Sky. The two guys, neither averse to tipping back endless shots of bourbon, hit it off as friends. As someone who did not drink alcohol, Buffy soon drifted away, leaving the two to while away their days over the bottle.[66]

A 1965 *Life* magazine feature article on Buffy noted her passion and versatility: "She will sing a quiet little love song. After that she will turn on her audience with sparks in her black eyes and shout out angrily in song about the injustices done to her people, or of the cruelty of war."[67] Buffy never wanted to be pigeonholed as a protest singer. She has written hundreds of songs—only a handful of which are protest songs. These, however, are so arresting they seemed to overshadow her other work.

Buffy's *Many a Mile* was released in 1965. Her first single release, the tender love song "Until It's Time for You to Go" on one side and "Apple Tree" on the other, was released by Vanguard in the United States and by Fontana in the United Kingdom. Fontana released a second single that year with "Universal Soldier" paired with the American folk classic "Cripple Creek." "Universal Soldier" is considered by many to have been Buffy's best composition. Glen Campbell recorded "Universal Soldier," and would later record "Until It's Time for You to Go" and "Take My Hand for Awhile."

By the age of twenty-four, Buffy had performed in the United Kingdom (playing at London's Royal Albert Hall), Australia, Canada, and Hong Kong. In Hong Kong she got a chance to spend time with famous martial artist Bruce Lee and other Chinese movie stars. Buffy was commanding up to $2,500 a concert, a significant amount for the times. Her powerful and multifaceted performances took the audiences by storm. A review in Melbourne described a fierceness and integrity that helped to take any song and lift it beyond routine levels. In Hong Kong, a reviewer called Buffy's high level of stage art as only one bend in a most extraordinary river. Regarding her travel experiences, Buffy once commented that she felt like she lived several lives in Europe and had a whole other life in Hong Kong.[68]

With her dizzying rise to popularity and strong demand from a young public for her albums, Buffy found herself suddenly doing very well financially. *Life* magazine reported that by 1965 she was earning over $100,000 per year (not bad, considering the dollar had about ten times today's purchasing power). "I may buy a ten-room house in either New England, Mexico, or Spain," she said, jokingly.

Wanting a break in the fall of 1965, Buffy vanished for three months, ending up on the small island of Formentera, east of Spain. She recalls it being a very isolated pastoral setting where ancient Roman wagon ruts were etched into the dirt roads, where ex-Nazis seemed to hide out, and where women in black robes pointed two fingers at you to give the "evil eye." On Formentera, Buffy found the quiet she needed to work on a concerto for guitar, some poetry, and her scathing song, "My Country 'Tis of Thy People You're Dying," which she intended as "Indian History 101" for her audiences.[69]

Despite her success, Buffy socially remained largely an outsider in Greenwich Village. In many ways she preferred it like that. The Village was a scene in which the most successful performers were those who actively pursued their business affairs, often in bars. Recalling those heady days, Buffy supposes that not networking impeded her career a lot. She was always a loner and was rather isolated as a musician.

"I didn't drink alcohol and that has been a hugely positive element in my personal life. But it has been a negative thing in terms of careerism. One is expected to go out and have a beer or some wine after a concert, especially in Europe. I'm a teetotaler not because I don't think people shouldn't drink, but I just don't like the taste. When I was first famous in Paris, someone would pull out this hundred-year-old bottle of wine. And I would say, 'Oh, no thank you.' You aren't supposed to say that! So there were certain things coming into show business that I was naïve about."

Buffy's naïveté proved costly in other ways, making her vulnerable to financial exploitation. "When I first went to

Greenwich Village, I had never met a businessman and never met a lawyer ... I had no idea that [show business] was about money. I thought it was about music. I played at the Gaslight and the Highwaymen heard "Universal Soldier." After my set, I went and sat with them ... and one of the people at the next table said, 'Yeah, we're going to record it. Who's the publisher?'"[70]

Buffy wasn't familiar with publishing and didn't realize how important it is in establishing one's legal ownership to a song. Elmer Gordon, who was at the next table, sensed her naïveté and spoke up right away, offering to do her a favour. He said he would help but that he would have to do it legally. Gordon wrote up a contract on the spot, told Buffy he had to give her a dollar to make it legal, and had Buffy sign it. She signed away the rights to "Universal Soldier" for $1. She didn't know better. In 1965 Scottish folksinger Donovan generated a lot of revenue when he marshaled the song into a top hit. It would take Buffy ten years and $25,000 to buy back the rights to her song.

John Kay, lead singer of Steppenwolf, recalls being inspired by Buffy to sing about things he felt strongly about. He saw her perform at the Troubador in Los Angeles between late summer of 1964 and early 1965. When Kay hitchhiked back east and began playing around Yorkville in Toronto, he saw her again at the Purple Onion. He was absolutely floored by her intensity, her incredible fervour. The closest thing to it that he had experienced to that point had been in the Black gospel community and in performances by Ray Charles or Little Richard, where the human voice became the carrier of sheer raw emotion. Seeing Buffy make such powerful statements in her songs encouraged Kay to do the same in his music.[71]

Perhaps it was because of this passion, so apparent in her performances, that Buffy was recruited by United Nations Children's Fund (UNICEF) to do concerts in "have" countries for the benefit of refugees from "have-not" countries. Buffy recalls that she travelled a lot for UNICEF with Harry Belafonte, Marlon Brando, Danny Kaye, Dinah Shore, Peter Ustinov, and the great flamenco guitarist Manitas de Plata. She also performed concerts for Save the Children and the UN High Commission for Refugees. She spent a lot of time travelling to Asia, Australia, New Zealand, and Scandinavia.[72] Although everyone was paid the same minimal amount (about $35 a day), Buffy found her overseas experiences to be immensely enriching.

Back at home in 1965, Buffy took to the stage at the Newport Folk Festival, along with other folk singers like Bob Dylan, Joan Baez, Gordon Lightfoot, Patrick Sky, and Pete Seeger. That year Dylan was booed by parts of the audience for expanding into electronic music. But already something about the atmosphere of the American music scene felt different. Traditional folk music somehow seemed to be losing its novelty, as well as the intimacy that made it unique.

Beatlemania, which had firmly taken hold in Britain, now captured America. On February 9, 1964, the band debuted on the *Ed Sullivan Show* to an unprecedented audience of 74 million people, almost half the American population. On a return visit in

1965, the Beatles played to an audience of 56,000 in Shea Stadium, the first major stadium concert in rock and roll history. Although many in the American media dismissed the group as a passing fad, the British group was the front end of a wave of popular music that would threaten to swamp the place enjoyed by folk musicians—a wave that would change the music scene forever.

American icon Elvis Presley had met the Beatles and didn't like what he saw: unkempt hair, antiwar lyrics, and use of drugs. In a 1970 meeting with President Richard Nixon, Presley suggested that the four be banned from entering the United States again.

Unlike many folk music singers, Buffy explored other genres from early on in her career. Her album *Many a Mile* included "The Piney Wood Hills," which was covered by top country singers; "Maple Sugar Boy" and "Broke Down Girl," both jazz pieces; and "Until It's Time for You to Go," a successful pop hit destined to become a standard. Despite pressure from folk music purists, Buffy herself preferred a flexible and diverse music scene. In 1966, she issued her third album, the popular *Little Wheel Spin and Spin*.[73]

Buffy was becoming very well known; part of that visibility meant that she was making the rounds of television appearances. Early 1966 was a busy junket of television performances for Buffy: she played herself on *To Tell the Truth*; she was interviewed on *The Merv Griffin Show* and performed on *The Andy Williams Show*. Her songs were increasingly popular with other musicians as well. Both Bobby Darin and singer and activist Nancy Sinatra recorded "Until It's Time for You to Go" that year.

In 1967, Buffy performed at Carnegie Hall in front of an audience of 2,400 people. Returning from a tour, the first act that Bob Dylan took in to reacquaint himself with what was happening in Greenwich Village was Buffy's performance at the Bottom Line.[74] Buffy maintained a gruelling schedule in those early years as a budding performer. Bill Raffee, who followed Buffy's career, said: "She has gone out alone on tours that would kill the average horse, armed only with her guitar and a canvas suitcase. She's arrived home at the end of the tour sick, tired, and broken-hearted, but any collection of reviews she's left behind will show that she strengthened the hearts of a hundred thousand strangers. I caught her crying in the snow one time after a big city concert that had been a study in power and delight and had left the audience ecstatic, on their feet, and begging for more at curfew time. I asked, what is the matter? She looked about four years old with the tears and the snow coming down and would only say, 'I just miss him sometimes.'"[75]

Raffee did not learn who "him" was. Buffy recalls that it was a reference to one of the Corbin kids with whom she became close. But Raffee was surprised at how she could, "in the blink of an eye forget it all, the lights, the music, the splendour, the applause, and turn back into a soft, vulnerable little girl."

I've damn near walked this world around
Another city, another town
Another friend to say goodbye

And another time to sit and cry
Ohhh it's many a mile I have spent on this road
It's many a mile I have gone
"Many a Mile," written by Patrick Sky, sung by Buffy Sainte-Marie

The first couple of years in Greenwich Village and Buffy's rise as a recording artist resulted in attention that went far beyond anything she could have imagined. All of her creative work and album production resulted in a steady whirlwind of activity. One observer noted: "I've travelled around after Janis Joplin, Tina Turner, Joan Baez, even the Beatles in their early days; and Buffy Sainte-Marie's effect on people astounds me, because I tell you, it is absolutely positive and entirely different from that of anyone I have ever seen. There is a sense of royalty about her, like royalty from a very funky, high primitive planet somewhere, but very definitely royalty. She is not one of the common people, though I have seen her try to be, and I don't really think that she is conscious that she can ever be, because she seems to feel left out instead of privileged. When Buffy Sainte-Marie enters a room, everybody feels it."[76]

Buffy's willingness to voice her antiwar music and Native American protest songs made her a controversial figure during a tumultuous time in America. It was the 1960s, when the baby boomers were making their influence felt. By 1967 Buffy needed a refuge from her sudden fame and she craved a quiet place where her creativity could be nourished. She would eventually find such a spot in a most unexpected locale.

CHAPTER 5

HAWAII:
A QUIET PLACE

＊

On January 20, 1778, Captain James Cook's expedition made its
first contact with the Hawaiian people on the islands of Kauai and
Niihau, the smallest inhabited islands in the chain. Cook came
upon a kingdom ruled by hereditary monarchs who owned all of
the land and passed it to their heirs. By 1810, Hawaii was unified
under Kamehameha the Great. American missionaries arrived
in 1820, bringing not only their religious but also their political
and social views. What took hundreds of years to evolve in
Europe happened very quickly in Hawaii. Responding to outside
influences, Kamehameha and his descendants transformed Hawaii
from a feudal society into a constitutional monarchy recognized
by other nations around the world.

However, history was about to conspire against the native
Hawaiians. Foreign interests and businesses were becoming
increasingly powerful. When Queen Lili'uokalani attempted to
restore the monarchy's weakened powers in 1887, the move was
interpreted as a threat to American business interests. This led to

a conspiracy to overthrow the monarchy and, on July 7, 1893, American naval forces occupied Hawaii on the pretext of protecting American citizens. U.S. Navy ships aimed their big American guns at Honolulu and the "bayonet constitution" effectively stole Hawaii from its people. By 1898 Hawaii was officially annexed to the United States.

Kauai, also called the Garden Isle, at just over 800 square km (500 sq. mi.) in area is geologically the oldest of the Hawaiian Islands. Kauai essentially has two seasons—rainy and not. Although it can rain nearly every day in Kauai, the steady rainy season is from November to March. Mount Wai'ale'ale, not far from where Buffy lives, carries the dubious reputation of being the rainiest spot on Earth as it receives up to 1168 cm (460 in.) of rain annually. All around the island, rainfall has carved out deep gorges with beautiful waterfalls, some of which can be seen from Buffy's farm. The island is especially prone to flooding during tropical storms and hurricanes. As of 2009, Kauai had about 65,000 permanent residents, but in the 1960s it was still unspoiled with a population closer to 25,000.

Buffy recounts how she came to discover Hawaii in 1966: "I had been travelling too much and at the moment I happened to have been based in Los Angeles for a few weeks. I was tired of travelling all the time, and the show business and interviews and fans and everything … It was acid time in L.A. and I needed a vacation. I was too famous for a while. As a new songwriter, I had too much money and not enough privacy. Enough is enough …

I just wanted to pull back, which is much more my nature than being out there sparkling and shining, which is fun but . . ."[77]

Buffy had some time off before her first and only concert in Honolulu. She decided to contact a travel agent and told her that she was going to be in Hawaii and wanted to take some time off and go where no one would know who she was. The agent recommended the outer islands, as Honolulu on Oahu was a big city. So Buffy decided to go to the outer island of Kauai. Once she set foot there, Buffy knew that this was where she wanted to stay forever.

The forests of Kauai, its abundant natural beauty and quiet, so far from civilization, appealed to her immediately. It would take her only four days to find the place she would come to love. "I went to this little island and I stayed in a bed and breakfast. I had been there one or two or three days and I had rented a car and drove by this place, like a real estate office, a little tiny shack. There was a white-haired man there named John Texiera. John was on the phone, but motioned me in, saying, Sit down, sit down, I'll make all your dreams come true in a minute!'"[78]

Buffy told Texiera she was looking for a really remote place to call her own. He was kind to her. She told him she had been living on a Christmas tree farm in the state of Maine and that did it. "Okay, I've got the place in mind," he said. Texiera drove Buffy to a property in the middle of nowhere on the slope of a mountain. It was also a Christmas tree farm and Buffy bought it on the spot!

Buffy's land was located halfway up a dormant volcano and not far from a forest reserve. The owner, Clair Bickle, had lived there for about thirty years and planted Norfolk pine trees, which he sold as Christmas trees in Hawaii. Buffy describes it as a quiet place in the mountains where you would never know it as Hawaii. There was no nearby beach; the scenery looked more like Alberta or Colorado.

Here, away from the busy music scene, was finally a spot where Buffy could relax and regenerate in the quiet she so sorely needed to continue her creative work. The terrain was verdant, with lush foliage fuelled by the heaviest annual rainfall in the world. Buffy was warned she would need a chainsaw to access the more heavily overgrown areas of her land. Several waterfalls could be seen in the distance after a heavy rain.

Buffy soon discovered the thrill of surfing, which she compared to beautiful music. She also discovered, fell in love with, and married (in 1968) her first husband, Dewain Kamaikalani Bugbee, a young blond surfer of part-Hawaiian descent. Bugbee was a few years younger than Buffy. His mother, Thelma Sproat Bugbee, was a well-respected Hawaiian elder, tennis player, and social worker. Buffy enjoyed spending time with Thelma, learning about the real Hawaii.

Buffy and Bugbee spent a few months ploughing, planting, and developing the new property. They acquired dogs, horses, and other animals, but Buffy was not able to remain there as much as they both hoped, due to her busy schedule. Bugbee tried touring with Buffy for the first couple of years of their marriage but eventually opted to remain home in Hawaii.

Buffy's farm is surrounded by thickets of hau trees (found all over Hawaii). Their branches grow low to the ground and tangle with one another. The bark of the tree is used by traditional Native Hawaiians to make cord that can be used for various purposes, including making baskets and sandals. The hau tree's delicate flower lasts for only one day, quickly turning from yellow to red to orange before dropping off. With about twelve metres (40 ft.) of rain per year, the hau trees become covered with moss. The ground is always damp and vegetation grows year round. Every season paths are cut through the underbrush. These trails lead to little nooks and crannies that provide what Buffy calls her "sacred spots."

Buffy gives away most of her Christmas trees, each of which grows a new top when the old top is cut down. She also sells some of the giant Norfolk pines. Artists make beautiful bowls out of the wood. The walls of the bowls are so thin they are translucent. Kauai art galleries have a wide selection of these beautiful blue and honey-coloured artworks.

Buffy's love for Hawaii has done wonders to inspire her art. She loves the sense of quiet, broken only by the sounds of crickets, birds, and other animals. The colour is rich and natural, and after a couple of days back in Hawaii, Buffy relaxes and is ready to write.

"It's like having a blank canvas. I've never understood people who say they get writer's block … I thrive in it … I thrive on an empty space to fill with creativity … I'm like a sponge; if I don't allow myself the space and time to fill up, I'll be trying to squeeze something out and there's nothing in there … So this place for me

Buffy with her first husband, Dewain Kamaikalani Bugbee

is where I can really be on input. And then when I go out on the road I have something to give that's a little bit more than just words and music. It's renewal, a thrill—I genuinely like to do this."[79]

Buffy was doing well financially, and this enabled her to do something to improve the welfare of Native American people, especially regarding education. One of Buffy's early acts after her move was to find a way to share her newfound wealth with needy Native American students. In 1969, she created the non-profit Nihewan Foundation. "Nihewan," a Cree word meaning "speak Cree," referred to her desire to revitalize the Cree culture. Recalling her own difficulty in finding the funds to go to university, Buffy generously gave out scholarships.

"I was just a young singer with too much money. I knew what I wanted to do with that money. It was very unusual and I didn't know if it could actually be done, but I set up the foundation to provide scholarships to Native American people to study anything they wanted. Later, I expanded it to include scholarship money for anyone of any background who wanted to study Native studies or go into some field benefitting Native people."[80] Although the foundation was founded primarily to assist American Indian students in pursuit of higher education, it also contributed funding to promote understanding about Native peoples by supporting Native American educators and disseminating information for the education of non-Native Americans.[81]

By 1975, the Nihewan Foundation had funded twenty-three students through their university studies. "The Nihewan Foundation is putting only Indian people through college. An Indian guy, just in having lived his twenty years as an Indian, has twenty years of 'Native education' on the non-Indian guy. He doesn't have to break down all the barriers. He knows what being an Indian is like. An Indian can't make it in the same position as a white can, not so much because of prejudice as because we don't have the connections. My money is going into the foundation to help people I know are interested. I'm putting people through college who cannot get scholarships from other sources. What we need are our own lawyers and judges in court. And everything else."[82]

One of the individuals helped by the foundation was Lionel Bordeaux from the Rosebud Reservation in South Dakota. Dr. Bordeaux obtained his PhD in educational administration from the University of Minnesota in 1973. A prominent leader in education, Dr. Bordeaux was the founding president of Sinte Gleska College (later University) in his home community. He also helped to create (and became president of) the American Indian Higher Education Consortium, an organization dedicated to securing funding and accreditation for the system of tribal colleges in the United States.

Another Nihewan scholarship recipient, Dr. Francis D. Becenti, studied tribal college leadership for his PhD at Colorado State University. In the late 1990s, he, too, became the president of a tribal college: Degandawitha-Quetzalcoatl University near Davis, California. Becenti was interim president of Dine College in Arizona when it hosted President Bill Clinton during a visit supporting increased technological access on Indian reservations.

Microsoft subsequently donated almost $3 million to Dine and other tribal colleges.

Says Buffy: "As the founder of an educational foundation that has, since the 1960s, given away millions of dollars to students who are trying to make the world better, healthier, smarter, I have seen scholarship recipients go on to great lives, including some who became college presidents. As a member of the World Indigenous Nations Higher Education Consortium, I work with other PhDs from New Zealand, Australia, and the Americas to create and sustain tribal colleges, and to pave students' paths from kindergarten to high school graduation ... I have won one of the greatest awards in the entertainment industry—the Academy Award's coveted Oscar. But it is not the greatest honour that I have received. That honour was reserved for the occasion when I learned that two recipients of my little Nihewan Foundation had gone on to become presidents of tribal colleges."[83]

Lawyer, rights activist, and close friend, Delia Opekokew, describes how she first met Buffy and helped her to establish a major American Indian cultural centre in the early 1970s: "I was the organizer of the concert at Convocation Hall in Toronto and invited Buffy to put on a benefit concert. It was very successful and we made money, which is very unusual in a charity concert. She phoned me out of the blue about a year later and invited me to come and work for her in New York City to get on this project that she was trying to get started.

"It was wonderful. We were in an office which she had rented in New York. And one of the acts was Ravi Shankar. Walking around with Buffy was exciting. We went to some of the coffee houses in Greenwich Village and people came up and talked to her. I remember one time ... this man ran up to her and said, 'Buffy,' and hugged her. She introduced me: it was Dick Gregory and he was a famous comedian at the time. And walking around with her in New York, people would approach her, knew her, and she was very gracious with them. She was obviously very well versed in music. It was an eye-opener for me."[84]

The project Buffy was trying to start when she met Opekokew was the Native American Center for the Living Arts in upstate New York. Buffy had already come up with the concept and the name: the actual project was developed and realized by Duffy Wilson, a Tuscarora sculptor, who Buffy had invited to participate in the initial brainstorm. Buffy brought together Native American artists of different tribal backgrounds and disciplines to discuss the idea of a museum and contemporary art show facility. The original concept included live performance, painting, sculpture, traditional and contemporary craftwork, and even gardens of Native American flowers, fruits, vegetables, and medicinal plants. Buffy invited American Indian artistic geniuses who would later become prestigious in world-class art—people such as Rupert Costo, Arthur Junaluska, Charles Loloma, Lloyd Oxendine, Rain Parrish, Fritz Schroeder, Bob Spoonhunter, Dennis Sun Rhodes, and John Trudell. Funding agencies, like the National Endowment for the Arts, the New York State Council on the Arts, and the New

York City Council on the Arts, were also approached.

Opekokew continues: "I used to meet with those people and it's only now later, as I become better read that I realize how important they were. That was the kind of environment Buffy was involved in. Working with Buffy made me focus and think, well, I should get some better education because I could do more with my life. The opportunity came the next year and I took it."[85]

The Native American Center for the Living Arts, a 5,575 sq. metre (60,000 sq. ft.) facility in the shape of a turtle, was completed in 1981 with the help of state and federal funding. Today the centre displays artifacts, holds craft fairs, and hosts Native dance performances, attracting 35,000 visitors per year.

Opekokew, now a lawyer in Toronto and the first woman ever to run for the leadership of the Assembly of First Nations, recalls her earliest impressions of Buffy: "The first memory I have of her songs when I used to play them extensively was in the 1970s. One song I loved is called "Guess Who I Saw in Paris?" ... a love song. Of course I loved "Now That the Buffalo's Gone." I thought that was just so heartfelt and thought-provoking.

"We were all activists in those days, and she really got the message and sent out the message from the perspective of Native youth at the time. She was very instrumental to the work ... we wanted to change the world, not only for ourselves, but for our people. Her singing was instrumental because she summarized it. As Buffy has said many times, one of the best ways to tell a story is to do it succinctly and short. She does it in three-minute songs."

Opekokew saw Buffy as being brutally honest. What Buffy gave young people like Opekokew as they were growing up was hope and a belief in themselves and a belief that they could have dreams and desires of what they could achieve as adults. Buffy encouraged them to believe it would be worth continuing to go to school and become someone who would be helpful.

Opekokew was impressed with Buffy's focus, including the manner in which Buffy took good care of her health while on tour: "I travelled to Washington, D.C. and to Cleveland because [Buffy] was doing a concert there. I went over to her room and knocked on her door. 'Oh,' she says, 'I was just in the middle of doing yoga.' I was just so impressed that she was so disciplined that she could do her yoga in the hotel room.

"The other thing about Buffy is that in the '60s and '70s, people used to party a lot. I remember that she just removed herself from that environment. She would ... focus on making sure that she put on a good show. If she needed a good night's sleep, she would make sure that she had a good night's sleep. She ate healthy. She was very much into discipline in order to give the best of herself, whatever she was doing."[86]

Buffy was known for her willingness to be involved in the causes and went out of her way to be of help to local Native communities. One friend, Albert Angus of the Thunderchild First Nation of west-central Saskatchewan, recalls how Buffy helped his community build a new school. Angus was a CBC broadcaster and his home community was protesting the fact that the federal government refused to build a new school to replace one that had burnt down five years earlier. When Chief Thunderchild signed Treaty Six in 1879, he was told there would always be a schoolhouse on his reserve.

The community had the idea of staging a benefit concert. When it came to selecting a performer, someone suggested contacting Delia Opekokew, who told Angus where to contact Buffy, and Angus sent a long telegram describing the issues and asking whether Buffy would be interested. One of Buffy's agents called Angus, asking if he could meet Buffy at a concert in Missoula, Montana. Angus managed to persuade a newspaper to buy him a plane ticket in return for filing a story.

Angus made it to Missoula just in time for her show, and halfway through the event, to Angus's delight, Buffy announced she was going to go to Saskatchewan to hold a benefit concert for Thunderchild.

The concert was arranged for August 18, 1975, in Saskatoon. Then, as fortune would have it, a strike shut down the venue. Buffy agreed to reschedule the event in her own community, the Piapot Reserve, in September. Two weeks after the concert, the government announced that they would build the school after all.[87]

Angus first met Buffy when he was an interviewer on the CBC show, *Our Native Land*. Angus later became an actor and then a lawyer. He is one of the friends Buffy cites as an example of the strides being made by the Saskatchewan Cree. Sometimes, Angus would stop by to check in on Buffy's dad, Emile. That was a great help and comfort to Buffy, who, far away in Hawaii, worried about her parents.

Kauai is one of the most remote places on Earth. Flying to Canada can be quite an ordeal. Upon leaving Kauai, a traveller might spend a two-hour layover in Honolulu before boarding a six-hour flight to Vancouver, or a six-hour direct flight to Los Angeles or San Francisco. When flying from the West Coast to Toronto, the traveller must add at least another five hours of air time. Jet lag is a fact of life.

Despite the distance, Buffy travelled to the mainland frequently. She worked on her fourth album, *Fire & Fleet & Candlelight*, and performed new songs at the 1967 Newport Folk Festival in Rhode Island, one of the most established of the music festivals. Other performers included Leonard Cohen, Judy Collins, Arlo Guthrie, Gordon Lightfoot, Joni Mitchell, and Pete Seeger. The atmosphere was mellow and the outlook for the future was optimistic.

Fire & Fleet & Candlelight was released in 1967. A flood of new songs followed between 1968 and 1973, presented in new albums, including *I'm Gonna be a Country Girl Again, Illuminations, She Used to Wanna be a Ballerina, Moonshot,* and *Quiet Places.*

Buffy appeared at a pop festival in Northridge, California, near Los Angeles, in June 1969. Jimi Hendrix, the electrifying guitarist, was the headline act but there were numerous stellar performers, including Eric Burden, Buddy Miles, the Byrds, Joe Cocker, Marvin Gaye, and Tina Turner. The event faced logistical problems:

inadequate food, water, and bathrooms, and some of the 200,000 partying fans became unruly. Buffy and other performers urged the crowd to remain calm and enjoy the music. It became too much for the Hell's Angels who provided security, and the police were called to help restore order. Fifteen police and 300 fans were treated for injuries. Buffy later lamented, "It was acid time in L.A."

The "love-in" atmosphere of music festivals came crashing down at the Altamont Music Festival, held near San Francisco later that year. The event was headlined by the Rolling Stones and included Crosby, Stills and Nash, the Grateful Dead, Jefferson Airplane, and Santana. The Hell's Angels motorcycle club was hired to perform security, reportedly for 500 cases of beer. Tension in the crowd was fuelled by alcohol and drugs, and when a biker's motorcycle was knocked over, pandemonium broke out. One fan died in the melee.

Buffy continued appearing on popular television talk shows, including Johnny Carson's *Tonight Show*, where she debuted on June 24, 1971, and again on March 6, 1972. She also appeared on *The Andy Williams Show*.

Buffy was also becoming famous internationally and was developing a taste for the different experiences to be found beyond North American borders. In 1972 she spent weeks in Hong Kong: "I'm living in China. My life is consisting of heavy physical martial arts training. I'm really feeling good from kung fu and it shows in my music. I'm playing well and feeling happy. The vibes I am getting from people are entirely different from American vibes.

People are talking to each other in different ways, or looking at each other with a look that's considered too intimate here.

"Or I'm living in France, drinking a lot of coffee, and playing the piano every day. And I'm feeling physically weak but intellectually strong. I'm reading a lot and speaking French, not even thinking in English anymore. People are touching and looking and nourishing each other in ways that are nothing like the American experience. What I basically learned is that there are more possibilities than I think most Americans are aware of."[88]

Having gained considerable international exposure, Buffy felt she needed to return to performing in the United States for American listeners. She was a huge hit internationally, but who knew her in America? "Not having performed in this country for a long time gave me the opportunity, challenge, and obligation to bring people up to date. You know, over here they still think of me in terms of 'Universal Soldier.' I'm really an international superstar and an American secret. I've had a lot of hot records, gold and silver albums in other countries that were hardly heard of in the States. I want to kind of fill people in on where they were at when I split and where we're all at now, because my old record company stopped distributing my stuff and the people got left behind."[89]

Buffy saw music and performing as her life and she expressed all of her emotions through music. Her family was her band and her marriage was to music. Buffy viewed music as a social lubricant and a healing force, and the stage as a holy place.[90]

She was living in Hawaii under an assumed name and only a

close circle of friends was aware of her true identity. She endured a fire at her house in Hawaii in the early 1970s that destroyed her early family photographs and other childhood keepsakes. There are equally destructive forces of a much different kind to endure on the island. Hurricanes tend to hit Hawaii about once every decade and, because of the islands' isolated location, the consequences can be severe. Hurricane Iwa struck Kauai on November 23, 1982, causing $234 million in damages. Buffy's house suffered a lot of damage that time.

Buffy loves her home and its natural environment, even though she has witnessed the occasional natural disaster. And, despite the calamities of life, this artist continues to create.

CHAPTER 6

SONGWRITING: SOMETHING TO SAY

As a teenager, Buffy had been in love with rockabilly and early rock 'n' roll: Buddy Holly, the Everly Brothers, Jerry Lee Lewis, Elvis Presley, and Little Richard. Her personal musical tastes were broad and that passion for variety never stopped. Folk music was becoming popular as Buffy emerged from university in 1962 and she discovered she was very good at entertaining fellow students as a "one man band" and songwriter. Buffy was spending most of her time on the road alone, her only tools a notebook, a portable guitar, and her songs.

Buffy always felt that she wouldn't last, that her presence in show business was accidental. She was just a "by-ear" guitar player but nobody in folk music was interested in knowing or understanding that. Buffy felt, though, that her songs had something to say—important messages that society ought to hear. Later, with the advantage of computers and able to afford a band, Buffy would surprise people by experimenting with and producing new sounds, and repackaging her ideas in new and appealing ways.

Buffy's debut album, *It's My Way!*, was released by Vanguard Records in 1964. The album's cover featured Buffy holding a mouthbow made for her by her friend and singer-songwriter Patrick Sky. Producer Maynard Solomon introduced Buffy's songs as "music-poetry" with a hint of blues inflection—a style difficult to pin down. He called her a poet, composer, and singer who weaved her craft together in a special way. Her unusual voice, he conjectured, must have had its origins somewhere in primitive society.

Solomon sensed Buffy's message was a universal one and that Buffy was not afraid to explore it: "It is with roads, paths and ways that Buffy Sainte-Marie is concerned. She does not take the easy way, the way of saying "no" to the world and all in it as an assertion of simple Bohemian freedom. Though she is a dissenter, she does not travel the road of spectacular dissidence. Though she sings of freedom, she does not exalt the illusory freedom of the naysayer. The way of Buffy Sainte-Marie cuts through pain to awareness, digs through the layers of human weakness to disclose the strengths of men, exposes what is in order to reveal what might be."[91]

Asked early on about her motivations for singing, Buffy affirmed that it was, basically, because she felt her songs had something to say. In a nutshell, her message was that "people don't have to accept unsatisfying modes of living. People today are largely unaware that there are alternatives to the ways that they don't like. I feel that I stand as an alternative." Indeed, Buffy was practising what she was preaching, leaving the stifling abuse and humiliations of her hometown for university and very independently making a life for herself. Thus the lyrics of the song "It's My Way," were apt: "I'm cutting my own way, through my own day, and all I dare say is it's my own."

Side one of *It's My Way!* featured three especially groundbreaking original compositions: "Now That the Buffalo's Gone," "Cod'ine," and "Universal Soldier." These were supplemented by her unique renditions of folk songs such as "The Old Man's Lament," "Ananias," and "Cripple Creek," as well as "Mayoo Sto Hoon," a reflection of Buffy's love for Eastern religions. "Now That the Buffalo's Gone" was the first widely-popular Native American protest song and was dedicated to Buffy's contemporary Peter La Farge. The lyrics object to the hypocrisy of Americans who lamented the nation's past injustices while allowing current ones, such as the building of Kinzua Dam in upstate New York. Her hit "Universal Soldier" was a powerful antiwar song that resonated during the unpopular Vietnam War.

The song "Cod'ine," is a lament of drug addiction (later recorded by Janis Joplin, Courtney Love, Quicksilver Messenger Service, and others) and the attempt to find redemption. "Cripple Creek," was simply a song "that was fun to play." Although Buffy's composition "Cod'ine" was often thought to have been composed by Donovan, Gram Parsons, and others, she is its sole creator. "Universal Soldier" has also been inaccurately attributed to Donovan.

The album title, *It's My Way!*, reflects Buffy's declaration of freedom from her earlier life. It signifies a determination to emerge into something better and uniquely her own. At the same time, the song of the same name warns those who might aspire to Buffy's life that it is not for all to follow:

I'm cutting my own way, through my own day,
And all I dare say is it's my own way. [...]

I can tell you things I've done
And I can sing you songs I have sung
But there's one thing I can't give
For I and I alone can live

The years I've known
And the life I've grown
Got a way I'm going and It's My Way

I got my own stakes in my own game
I've got my own name and It's My Way
I've got my own path that only I can go,
I've got my own sword in my own hand,
I've got my own plan that only I can know,

Don't be crying, don't be sighing,
Your day will come, your day alone,
Years you'll know and a life you'll grow,
You got a way to go and it's all your own
—Abridged from "It's My Way"

It's My Way! was a huge success. However, when Buffy arrived in England, she was in for a big surprise. Vanguard's United Kingdom distributor had tinted the record cover red and gotten involved in a lot of gimmickry about Red Indians. The UK distributor and most other British record company people thought it a logical move to distinguish Buffy's heritage from that of people from India. Some people still occasionally refer to Buffy as a "Red Indian." Vanguard supported her concern and suggested that, in future, the UK team use the same covers as the Americans. Although Buffy did not make a big deal about the incident, it never sat well with her. She thought that pumping up her Native American image with stereotypes in an attempt to sell records was unfair to Indigenous peoples, unnecessary, and unfairly downgraded her worth as a serious and versatile artist.

Buffy's second album, *Many a Mile*, was released in 1965. Its title song was a Patrick Sky composition. The album featured Buffy's own original compositions, Native American protest songs, passionate love songs, jazz songs, and lullabies, plus a bit of traditional folk, all with fearlessly expressive vocals and diverse styles of guitar playing, ranging from Delta blues to flamenco.

The album's most famous song was "Until It's Time for You to Go," an unexpected hit that would be sung again and again over the years by hundreds of artists, including Elvis Presley, Celine Dion, Barbra Streisand, and Chet Atkins. Another song, "Los Pescadores," came to Buffy when she was watching a group of fishermen hauling nets out of the ocean during a trip to Mexico.

"Groundhog" featured Buffy's mouthbow playing, and "The Piney Wood Hills," which later became a hit for country singer Bobby Bare, was a tribute to the forests of Maine where Buffy found both solitude and solace.

Buffy was initially judged on the basis of her first two albums, which reflected contemporary folk roots and included many of the songs that made her popular on the university circuit and, later, the New York coffee house scene. The protest song "Universal Soldier" touched the raw nerve of a public in the midst of the controversial Vietnam War, while "Cod'ine" resonated with the seemingly drug-obsessed youth counterculture. As well, Buffy's appearance as an outspoken and articulate Native American public figure took many people by surprise. Buffy became known for her brand of truthful and reflective songs. She also brought with her a charm and poise that radiated throughout her performances.

Although Buffy was generally heralded as a folksinger, she herself did not agree. Buffy appreciated folk music and the tradition that it preserved. But folk singers generally tended to be socially conservative. Buffy was outspoken and critical of the system. She was also highly creative and did not want to sing in only one style. Moreover, she hated the unimaginative clothes folksingers wore: "I hated commercial folk music, the Kingston Trio and all that commercial stuff. I didn't want what they were marketing as folk music. I didn't call myself a folksinger—other people called me a folksinger ... After a while you get purists. Are you a folksinger or not?' they would ask. I didn't really care. As a songwriter I write a lot of different styles of music. I would sometimes be embarrassed because some of my songs sounded like country songs or some were protest songs."[92]

Many people objected and some were upset with her. Buffy did not care. In 1966, her third album, *Little Wheel Spin and Spin*, was distinguished by several songs with similar guitar tunings to those Buffy introduced on her first album in "Cod'ine." The title cut was wrapped in that mesmerizing sound and contained cutting lyrics about hypocrisy:

Merry Christmas, Jingle Bells
Christ is born and the devil's in hell
Hearts they shrink, pockets swell
Everybody know and nobody tell
Little Wheels Spin and Spin
And the big wheels turn around and around ...
Blame the angels, blame the fates,
Blame the Jews or your sister Kate
Teach your children how to hate
And the big wheels turn round and around [...]
"Little Wheel Spin and Spin"

The song "Little Wheel Spin and Spin" reflects the same moral dilemma Buffy sang about in "Universal Soldier": that we all contribute by our own little acts to the big problems that terrify us, like little gears turning the bigger ones. One fan described the song as undulating with electrifying power that sent shivers up and down his spine as Buffy sang in her distinctive trembling voice, "Add your straw to the camel's load / pray like hell when your world explode."

Other songs on the album included "My Country 'Tis of Thy People You're Dying," and the haunting love song "Winter Boy." This album is diverse in terms of style, and, research scholar that she was, Buffy gave each song its own uniqueness, letting song dictate style. *Little Wheel Spin and Spin* cracked *Billboard's* Top 100.

Buffy had been touring in the United Kingdom prior to recording the album and heard some old traditional story ballads that she loved. Her renditions of "Sir Patrick Spens," "House Carpenter," "Lady Margaret," and "Waly, Waly" are intensely her own and revered among lovers of British folk songs. Completely different from these, and also much loved by Buffy, is "Rolling Log Blues," by Black blues singer Lottie Kimbrough. This diversity of music styles was something still welcome in the early 1960s. However, by the latter part of the decade, artists were being slotted into manageable categories such as country, bluegrass, blues, ethnic, and pop, so rarely did all styles appear on one album.

Toward the end of the 1960s, with the "British invasion" and the first manned landing on the moon, the music tastes of the Baby Boom generation changed. The coffee and pot of the early 1960s encouraged conversation, debate, and love-ins. But by the end of the decade, that innocence was corrupted by hard drugs and alcohol. Many coffee houses began getting liquor licenses.

The folk music era and its intellectual bent were out of favour. Folk artists, such as Bob Dylan and Joni Mitchell, explored other genres like rock and jazz.

Buffy's fourth album, *Fire & Fleet & Candlelight*, came out in 1967 and was again quite diverse, reflecting the increasing amount of travel that Buffy was doing overseas. Four of the album's songs were true folk songs: "Reynardine," "Lyke Wake Dirge," "Doggett's Gap," and "Lord Randall." Eight songs were Buffy originals and two were Joni Mitchell songs, as Buffy had been trying very hard to use her own fame to leverage her friend Joni's music. In a couple of songs, Buffy used a full rock band backup with session men Bruce Langhorn on electric guitar, Alexis Rogers on drums, and Russ Savakus on bass. These "rock" songs were Joni Mitchell's "The Circle Game" and Buffy's "97 Men in This Here Town Would Give Half a Grand in Silver Just to Follow Me Down." The album included the passionate sounds of "Summer Boy" and "Little Boy Dark Eyes."

Some critics felt that *Fire & Fleet & Candlelight* marked a betrayal of Buffy's folk music and her Native American roots and was, therefore, inconsistent. Buffy was never interested in "consistency" or keeping songs simply because they sounded like others. She valued originality and versatility. Her musical impact and unique Native American presence were striking enough to earn her a performance at the prestigious Carnegie Hall in 1967. She would appear there again with Johnny Cash and Chuck Berry. Later, in 1967, she toured Britain with Paul Simon.

In 1968, Buffy was invited by music producer and performer

Chet Atkins to record in Nashville. The city was well known for its Grand Ole Opry and Country Music Hall of Fame, but Nashville was becoming noted worldwide for the diversity of its performers and its music publishing. Although Nashville's reputation was built on country music, in fact, it was also a centre for Christian music, pop, rock, and, to a lesser extent, jazz.

Atkins loved talented people and good songs, and he played an important role in attracting talent to Nashville. He paid particular attention to the changing tastes in music and was quick to realize country music's need to make the crossover into rock and pop. This resulted in the new "Nashville sound." Atkins was a virtuoso guitarist and, later, RCA Records operations manager. He signed and/or worked with a multitude of artists, including Dolly Parton, Elvis Presley, Charley Pride, and Willie Nelson.

Buffy continued to explore her own creative freedom. In 1968, she recorded her fifth album, *I'm Gonna Be a Country Girl Again* (and dedicated it to Atkins) with some of Nashville's most beloved country music sidemen—Floyd Cramer, Junior Husky, Grady Martin, and Charlie McCoy—an experience she greatly enjoyed. Atkins produced the sessions but told Buffy at the start that, because he was signed to RCA, he could not be credited. The album included the love songs "Soulful Shade of Blue" and "Sometimes When I Get to Thinkin'." "I'm Gonna be a Country Girl Again," a song dedicated to nature and the countryside, was further popularized by singers Bobby Bare, Glen Campbell, George Hamilton IV, and Dottie West.

Because of Atkins's kind friendship, Buffy met many artists, including Johnny Cash, Floyd Cramer, Grady Martin, Dolly Parton, and Marty Robbins. Atkins also brought her together with young songwriters like Mickey Newberry and Kris Kristofferson. In 1969, Buffy appeared on *The Johnny Cash Show*. Johnny disclosed to Buffy that he "had part-Cherokee blood," then together they sang a rousing rendition of Peter La Farge's song "Custer."

Buffy was incorporating a broader spectrum of musical modes into her recordings. "I'm Gonna be a Country Girl Again" was a joyous country production number. "Until It's Time for You to Go" was a simple solo love song that would prove to become her greatest hit. Buffy said she could produce these diverse types of songs because each came from a different part of her experience. She actually felt all those different song emotions.

"My music has grown, but spherically. All the things I was doing years ago, I'm still doing. The reasons for living were valid to me then and are still valid to me now. "Generation" is an expansion of "My Country 'Tis of Thy People You're Dying," which is an extension of "Now That the Buffalo's Gone." "Moratorium" is an extension of "Universal Soldier," and so on."[93]

Although Buffy's title song cracked *Billboard's* Top 100, the album itself did not reach the sales of some of her previous ones. Fans and critics continued to see Buffy's versatility as a departure from what they considered her folk and Native American protest songwriting roots; some fans accused her of selling out. Others misperceived Nashville as being a redneck town. One critic was horrified that Buffy re-recorded "Now That the Buffalo's Gone" with what he surmised must be "a bunch of rednecks." Buffy defended Atkins's musicians against the slander, informing people that the musicians themselves had requested to perform the song on her *Country Girl* album and that they were as concerned as she was about Native American issues.

Buffy returned to Nashville again and again, where she always felt at home as a songwriter.

I'm gonna be a country girl again,
With an old brown dog and a big front porch and rabbits in the pen;
I tell you all the lights on Broadway don't amount to
an acre of green,
And I'm gonna be a country girl again.
"I'm Gonna Be a Country Girl Again"

Buffy's sixth album, *Illuminations*, launched in 1969, reveals her interest in experimenting with electronic instruments, including synthesizers and early computers. It was a highly successful effort that opened and closed with the immortal words from Leonard Cohen's critically praised *Beautiful Losers*, "God is alive, magic is afoot." Buffy worked with innovative sound engineer Michael Czajkowski of the New York University School of Arts to produce *Illuminations*. The album was reputed to be the first totally quadraphonic, electronic, vocal album and was technically way ahead of its time. All of the sound effects were created from Buffy's voice or guitar playing. The Buchla synthesizer

Cover art for *Illuminations*

processed the psychedelic sound of Buffy's hard rock song, "Better to Find Out Yourself," a rare effect for the time. The synthesizer also enhanced the impact of songs such as "He's a Keeper of the Fire." The ethereal other-worldly effect of "God Is Alive, Magic is Afoot" was especially noteworthy. While the album developed an almost-cult following among art students and lovers of electronic exotica because of its innovative sound, most folkies didn't get it.

Many of Buffy's hardcore fans were still unaccustomed to seeing her in anything more than her Native American role. The initial release of *Illuminations* saw weak sales and a decision was made to discontinue it. However, in 2000, *The Wire* magazine singled out *Illuminations* as one of the "100 albums that set the world on fire" because of its influence on artists over the next thirty years.[94]

In a 1969 review, Ralph Gleason of the *San Francisco Chronicle* raved about Buffy's versatility and how she made a successful transition from folk to other genres without abandoning the folk road completely: "To begin with Buffy Sainte-Marie can swing. She is a jazz fan and a listener to singers such as Billie Holiday and she can swing. Folk music generally does not swing in a jazz sense at all ... Buffy uses her voice as a musical instrument ... to be specific she uses it like an electric guitar, making glissandos and other electric-like sounds in a series of exchanges with the guitarist. This is really a jazz technique and it is remarkably effective when Buffy uses it ... on her blues songs, she takes the form of the blues ... then she creates lyrics that are not at all in the blues genre ... instead she writes modern poetry and sings it to the blues ... I suspect Buffy Sainte-Marie will break through the confines of folk music and become a major pop star and hit maker."[95]

Michigan Daily reviewer Bert Stratton also marvelled at Buffy's changeability: "She has a voice that is more resilient than any other female folk singer. The direction in which Buffy led those talents last night is impossible to pinpoint, in fact she's about the most eclectic singer there is. Buffy likes variety. She wasn't about to let me and the other veteran folkies in the audience meander in nostalgia for too long ... When Buffy could have conceivably gotten lost in the mélange she had created, she always brought it back home with a rootsy American-earth song. When she was finished her performance she was truly at home: a standing ovation from the sell-out crowd—encore—standing ovation—encore—and she was done."[96]

In 1971, Maynard Solomon of Vanguard Records called Buffy and said that music composer Jack Nitzsche wanted to record with her. Having been a philosophy major at the University of Massachusetts, Buffy was well acquainted with the work of the European philosopher Friedrich Nietzsche, who turned out to be Nitzsche's grandfather's brother (Nitzsche's mother had reportedly changed the spelling of their last name to distance the family from the great philosopher's controversial reputation).

In recording with Buffy, Nitzsche called upon his friend Ry Cooder, whom Buffy adored for his work in country blues, and Buffy's friend Taj Mahal, Cooder's bandmate in the Rising Sons. A Kiowa Indian, Jesse Ed Davis, was the third member of that band. Nitzsche also hired members of Neil Young's Crazy Horse band. Nitzsche had once said that when he saw Buffy's picture in *Cashbox* magazine, he instantly fell in love with her. He loved the diversity of her writing and her *Illuminations* album and felt that he could strengthen her rock sound. The haunting, other-worldly quality of her songs, such as "Poppies," entranced him.

Nitzsche began his career as an apprentice to Phil Spector, who developed the "Wall of Sound" technique in pop music. It was Nitzsche who first used big string orchestras in rock records. He also played keyboard for the Rolling Stones. The result can be heard in the production of Buffy's seventh album, *She Used to Wanna Be a Ballerina*, which came out in 1971. As usual for Buffy, the mix of songs was all over the place. The L.A. rock style was not her favourite; she much preferred a Deep South Delta rock, but producer Nitzsche made it work. Buffy's song "Now You've Been Gone for a Long Time" was a perfect Nitzsche dream come true in his capacity as a film composer, akin in style to some of Buffy's compositions on *Little Wheel Spin and Spin, Fire & Fleet & Candlelight,* and *Illuminations.*

Earlier in 1971, Buffy had been asked by Ralph Little, director of the just-completed movie *Soldier Blue*, to write a title song. Buffy turned the opportunity down twice but then a melody popped into her head that she liked. She called Little and said she'd do it. *Soldier Blue* depicts the 1864 Sand Creek Massacre, when the U.S. Cavalry attacked and massacred an unarmed Cheyenne and Arapaho village in the Colorado Territory. *Soldier Blue* was the first film ever to deal with the genocide of North American Indians and was quickly taken out of American theatres. Buffy's title song, "Soldier Blue," was orchestrated in England by Roy Budd and became a hit on the United Kingdom singles chart. The movie was hugely popular throughout Europe and Asia but was released just after the My Lai Massacre, hitting a raw nerve with the Vietnam War-obsessed American public, and gaining less exposure in the U.S. than had been hoped.

Working with Jack Nitzsche was a mixed blessing for Buffy. He drank a lot and could sometimes be volatile. Buffy felt Nitzsche had an unhealthy obsession with her. Even after the album was finished, he would call her at all hours at her home in Hawaii but Buffy displayed no interest. Her marriage to Dewain Bugbee was still on firm ground, despite his preference for staying home with friends rather than keeping up with Buffy's gruelling tour schedule.

During this time, Buffy was busy travelling, performing concerts, and being active in the American Indian movement. In her downtime she wrote, painted, danced, and hung out with friends on Indian reservations. Time spent with family at the Piapot Reserve, especially her grade-school-aged nieces and nephews, and return trips to her tree farm in Hawaii helped Buffy remain mellow and keep her sanity in the midst of the pandemonium of her professional life.

Buffy's urge to create new songs continued to press strongly. She was eager to record and wanted to return to Nashville to be among great musicians again. When she called Chet Atkins to ask about finding her the right producer, Atkins introduced her to bass player Norbert Putnam, from Muscle Shoals, Alabama. Putnam, with piano player David Briggs, had founded the band, Area Code 615 and the Quadraphonic Sound Studios in Nashville.

The Quadraphonic studio was an adapted old house with the control room in the porch and drums in the kitchen. Putnam was a Nashville fixture and one of the busiest pop/rock bassists in town. He played bass on some of Elvis Presley's albums and eventually become one of Nashville's most successful producers.

One contemporary called Putnam the hotshot producer of the time, able to play the role of producer, engineer or mixer as called for. He helped produce Joan Baez's album *Blessed Are ...*, which included the hit "The Night They Drove Old Dixie Down," a song written by Robbie Robertson. Putnam also worked with other top singers, including Jimmy Buffett, for whom he produced "Margaritaville," and Dan Fogelberg.

Buffy recalls these sessions as among the most enjoyable of her life. "I sure had a good time playing with Norbert Putnam's group at Quadraphonic Studios! I just loved it. I always loved Norbert's approach to music because he's the only one in music who's ever expressed it in the way of appreciating the artist's emotions. When the emotional integrity is there, the heart-touching part of a song and the singer singing a song, and the band are all on the same emotional page—it's very beautiful and I always appreciated it.

"They had a console, the actual machine that controls the instruments going on each track as it's recorded. They had one that they were getting ready to retire. I had my paints with me, glow-in-the-dark paints. I just started painting the little console. By the time we finished, the whole thing was all painted and everyone thought Norbert and I were both crazy. Recording at Quadrofonic was the most fun I'd ever had!"[97]

Buffy's eighth album, and first with Putnam, was *Moonshot*. It featured Putnam on bass, David Briggs on keyboards, Kenny Buttrey on drums, and a cast of Putnam's friends on guitars, including the famous Memphis Horns. Accomplished music

Cover art for *Moonshot*

engineer Gene Eichelberger took care of technical aspects. *Moonshot* included the songs "He's an Indian Cowboy in the Rodeo" (which reached number one on Boise, Idaho, radio in 1973), "Native North American Child," and "Mister Can't You See," the latter two reaching the Top 40. The song "Moonshot" has a haunting lyric about so-called primitivism versus modern progress: "See all the wonders that you leave behind / The wonders humble people own

/ I know a boy from a tribe so primitive / He can call me up without no telephone." Her own favourites from the *Moonshot* album are "Jeremiah," "Lay It Down," and her cover of the Elvis Presley B-side rockabilly song by Arthur Crudup, "My Baby Left Me."

The album cover for her ninth album, 1973's *Quiet Places*, features the verdant background of a Hawaiian landscape that tourists rarely see. *Quiet Places* included, among others, the rockabilly/roots Mickey Newberry song "Why You Been Gone So Long," as well as two of Buffy's most beautiful love songs: "No One Told Me" and "Clair Vol's Young Son."

Buffy's relationship with Dewain Bugbee had not turned out as well as she had hoped. He was not cut out to live the helter-skelter life of a famous singer. Their marriage lasted six years. Reflecting on the experience, Buffy mused, "We were very happily married and we are very happily divorced. I was hardly there anyway. He was a Hawaiian who liked to stay home and I was a musician who liked to travel."[98]

In 1974 Vanguard put together a compilation, mainly of her Native-focused songs, to comprise a tenth album, *Native North American Child: An Odyssey*. Buffy had not approved the album— she never liked it or the cover photo Vanguard used. However, turning lemons into lemonade, Buffy used its royalties to raise funds for Native American activist causes. The album included "Now That the Buffalo's Gone," "He's an Indian Cowboy in the Rodeo," "Soldier Blue," "My Country 'Tis of Thy People You're Dying," "Isketayo Sewow (Cree Call)," and "Way, Way, Way."

Buffy had become frustrated with Vanguard Records. "I was so green when I arrived in New York. I had never even met a lawyer, or a businessman for that matter. Vanguard wanted to sign me but I didn't have a lawyer, so they said I could use theirs and I did—an obvious conflict of interest. Years later my attorney, Abe Somer, pointed this out to me but for years I'd not known it. Vanguard put out so many albums using tracks I'd have considered out-takes. If only I had some artistic control, I would have at least used the takes that I'd liked. With Vanguard, I had none."[99]

When she refused to re-sign with Vanguard, the record company decided to strong-arm her. She was in the hospital with a gastric ulcer and Vanguard's art director, Jules Halfant, appeared at her bedside with a photograph she loathed in which her hair was green. Halfant told Buffy that if she re-signed she could control the picture; otherwise Vanguard would release an album with the hated picture and call it a "best of" album. Buffy refused to re-sign. Her last albums with Vanguard were *The Best of Buffy Sainte-Marie, Volumes 1 and 2*, a double-LP set comprising songs from her previous albums. Vanguard asked for no input whatsoever from Buffy and she hated both albums. They were a moderate success, drawing upon her earlier fame, and would later become the first of Buffy's early albums to be rereleased on CD by Lawrence Welk's company, the Welk Music Group (which bought out Vanguard Records in 1986.)

Buffy was disappointed again and again by her lack of control over Vanguard's choices of takes, photos, and decisions to keep reissuing old albums. By the end of 1974, Buffy had switched from Vanguard, the only recording company she had ever worked with, to MCA Records, one of the big players in the music business.

In the meantime, Buffy's friendship with Norbert Putnam had developed into a romantic relationship. They co-produced her albums *Buffy* and *Changing Woman*, while living together—they were inseparable.

Buffy included original songs, such as "Star Boy," which she had written in Hong Kong; two hot rockers, "Sweet Fast Hooker Blues" and "Sweet Little Vera"; and "Generation," a precursor to the powwow rock style she would continue to develop, and featuring quotes she remembered from Emile Piapot regarding the moon landing:

> *And me I don't wanna go to the moon*
> *I'm gonna leave that moon alone*
> *I just wanna dance with the Rosebud Sioux this summer.*
> *"Generation"*

Changing Woman emphasized Putnam's Deep South, electric, Muscle Shoals sound and included more remarkable original songs. "Eagle Man/Changing Woman" reflects Buffy's experience of the spiritual perspectives of Native America before colonization and yet still sounds futuristic, with her layered vocals providing a shimmering, ever-changing texture. The beautiful "Nobody Will Ever Know It's Real But You" is a love song written with Putnam (who wrote the music). Buffy sings it in a uniquely pure soprano, unusual for her. "Mongrel Pup," on the other hand, is as experimental as anything she had done on *Illuminations* as she multi-tracked various versions of her voice singing, talking, whispering, and shouting the lyrics—a very brave and original thing to do in the 1970s—foreshadowing the Eurythmics years later. Without seeing the album cover, few would guess it was Buffy Sainte-Marie.

And Baby she's a mongrel pup
Hybrid mutant girl
cross-bred nomad stronghead
and happy in the big bad world
We are the Space Age Council of
Intertribal Straight Ahead
And maybe you're a mongrel pup.
"Mongrel Pup"

The 1974 MCA album entitled *Buffy* had actually been recorded before *Quiet Places* was released by Vanguard. Buffy waited several months after breaking with Vanguard until contracting with MCA to release *Buffy*.

Buffy wrote some highly successful songs generic enough for any singer in the world to present to their own audiences. Her love song "Until It's Time for You to Go" is her most famous and successful. When Buffy wrote the tune, it was the last one she thought would become famous.

Buffy recalls how "Until It's Time for You to Go" was written: "This song popped into my head while I was falling in love with someone I knew couldn't stay with me ... "Until It's Time for You to Go" is about leaving space in your life for life to happen ... The bridge to the song is very, very different; I remember Chet Atkins eventually told me and so did somebody else—perhaps it was Cannonball Adderley—one of the jazz greats, that they had never heard that chord progression before. Da, da, da, da ... 'then, don't ask why,' but the base line goes up then it goes way down then it comes up again ... Bobby Darin was the first one to cover it."[100]

Buffy admits that, of all her songs, "Until It's Time for You to Go" is the one she enjoys singing the most, but one she has rarely heard played as she wrote it (with that unique progression of chords.) Buffy felt that Bobby Darin's musical director missed the chords in his rendition, and therefore so did Elvis (who included the song on fifteen albums) and the other Las Vegas singers who learned it from Darin's record. Darin's rendition made the song sound sadder than the way Buffy liked it. To Buffy, the song is one of joy in the unexpected—people can live together, even if just for a moment. "Until It's Time for You to Go" has been covered worldwide by hundreds of artists, including Petula Clark, Cher, Bobby Darin, Roberta Flack, Neil Diamond, Celine Dion, Willie Nelson, Nancy Sinatra, and Barbra Streisand.

When Elvis Presley heard "Until Its Time for You to Go," he thought it was perfect to dedicate to his wife, Priscilla. He sang the masculine lyrics that Bobby Darin had used:

I'm not a dream, I'm not an angel, I'm a man,
You're not a queen, you're a woman, take my hand,
We'll make a space in the lives that we'd planned
And here we'll stay, until it's time for you to go
Yes, we're different, worlds apart, we're not the same
We laughed and played at the start, like in a game
You could have stayed outside my heart, but in you came
And here you'll stay until it's time for you to go
Don't ask why, don't ask how,
Don't ask forever, love me now
This love of mine, had no beginning, it has no end
It was an oak, now I'm a willow, I can bend
And though I'll never in my life see you again
Still I'll stay until it's time for you to go
"Until It's Time for You to Go"

Buffy recalls that during a recording session at Quadrafonic in Nashville, the phone rang and it was one of Presley's business guys, who said, "Buffy, Elvis just recorded your song 'Until It's Time for You to Go.' Sounds great!" Buffy was flattered that her one-time idol had covered her song but there was more to the call than congratulations and flattery. The businessman continued, "Honey, we're going to have to have a piece of that publishing money."

Buffy didn't hesitate to say "no" right away. She had learned to hold onto the rights to her songs when she had given away the rights to "Universal Soldier" years before and she wasn't going to do it again, even for Elvis. Somebody from Elvis's camp would call her up about every six months: "It's Elvis and Priscilla's love song. He wants to do it in Vegas, but we're going to have a cut of that money." Next, they said they wanted to put it in a movie if she agreed, but still Buffy didn't budge. "No, I can't do it, I never will," she told them.

Elvis kept on recording it, singing it on tour, and put it in the movie anyway. "There was me, Little Miss Earnest, telling them royalties are the only money that a songwriter gets. You guys have all that other money, which is all right. My song was already famous before Elvis sang it." Buffy never did give in, and the royalties from that song turned out to be what, more than anything else, allowed her to survive as a full-time artist without having to get another job.[101]

Eventually Buffy and Putnam's creative partnership ran its course and they went their separate ways. Buffy signed with ABC Records at the request of Artie Mogul, the man who had discovered Peter, Paul and Mary, Bob Dylan, and Bill Cosby, and who was a big fan of hers. Her next album (the fourteenth), *Sweet America*, was again dedicated to and in support of American Indian activism. Buffy seemed to finally discover her unique style, producing the first example of "powwow rock." Powwow singing had not been combined with rock/pop music before and it was a fitting tribute to her Cree roots. Her classic, "Starwalker," and other songs like "Qu'Appelle Valley, Saskatchewan" and "I Been Down" are unabashedly Native American in theme and sound and so were popular with American Indian fans. *Sweet America* also included the hard-hitting rocker "Look at the Facts," the folksy acoustic "I Don't Need No City Life," and the gentle kids' poem by Eugene Field that Buffy set to music as "Wynken, Blynken and Nod." Her contract with ABC was to be short-lived, however, as ABC ran into financial difficulties and was eventually absorbed by MCA. *Sweet America* would be her last album until she began recording again after a fifteen-year break.

Buffy's songs were increasingly covered by other artists. Many of her songs have been recorded by all kinds of artists—there have been hundreds and hundreds of covers of "Until It's Time for You to Go." "Cod'ine" has been performed by fifteen other artists, including Janis Joplin and Courtney Love. "Universal Soldier" was so widely popularized by Scottish singer Donovan (one of his albums is also named *Universal Soldier*) that many people believed it was he who wrote the song. Donovan also included "Cod'ine" on five of his albums.

Buffy's "Up Where We Belong," co-written with Jack Nitzsche and Will Jennings, is her next most covered song, with nearly twenty singers providing their own renditions. Joe Cocker's duet with Jennifer Warnes for the movie *An Officer and a Gentleman* reached number one on the *Billboard* charts in 1982. Buffy, Nitzsche, and Jennings each scored Oscars for Best Song that same year.

Another love song, "Take My Hand for Awhile," was recorded by Glen Campbell, Francoise Hardy, George Hamilton IV, and others. The lyrics, "Take my hand for a while, explain it to me once again, just for the sake of my broken heart," are understandable to anyone who's ever known heartbreak.

Over her career Buffy has written more than 200 songs, recorded eighteen albums, and been recorded by more than 200 artists in sixteen languages. She has a devoted following. Buffy derives great pleasure from the feelings she gets from singing, nevertheless she has always considered herself first and foremost a songwriter, sometimes with a message to convey.

"I don't think of myself as a folk singer or an ethnic singer or a pop singer or any of those things. I just sing what I have to sing and people seem to like it. I don't think it's necessary to have a word for it. I've written several hundred songs and a few of them deal with Indian rights. One more is a protest song called "Universal Soldier." I've written a love song that is being released this week. As I say, I don't stick to one kind of music. I've written rock 'n' roll songs, and bluegrass songs, and country and Western songs, and lots and lots of love songs, and jazz songs.[102]

"I'm a singer-composer. Out of all the songs I've written, I've only written three songs that could be termed protest songs. "Universal Soldier" and the two that are dealing with Indian affairs are protest songs. I'm primarily an artist, which I think is a little bit different from being just an entertainer. I'm very serious about what I do, even if it is a funny song. My point is not just to distract someone. When a person leaves my concert, I want him to feel that he's been somewhere, he's been right inside those songs, he's lived those things. I still take a little bit of time out of each concert to inform people about Indian issues."[103]

As a songwriter, Buffy has an irrepressible and contagious enthusiasm that has reverberated throughout her adult life. "I'm kind of like a fountain spouting off and if somebody's there to enjoy it then that's good, but if they're not, I'm still going to spout. When I was a child I made up my songs and nobody listened. When I was a teenager, I didn't sing them because I was shy, but I still made them up. I haven't changed that much since then, inwardly anyway."[104]

Buffy is inspired by passionate and/or socially aware singers. Her early influences include Carmen Amaya, the great flamenco dancer, who was also a natural singer with incredible passion in her voice. Someone once said that Amaya sang from the soles of her feet. Buffy lived for a time in Spain with a Gypsy painter, where she was inspired by Amaya's talent as a flamenco dancer and appreciated her as a movie actress.

Buffy was also enamoured of the singing of Edith Piaf. "Oh, I get chills today—that voice and that passion coming from that person. That was how I felt, too. I didn't sing like that but I felt like that. I mean, she was, you know, they called her a street urchin. But whom did she take singing lessons from? The body, right? And it all came right from her. And what it did was it gave me permission to feel that deep and not to worry about vibrato or anything else but the song.

"That kind of passion just comes from your heart. And the sound just comes from opening the body. It's like jumping off a cliff—you don't know where the note's going to land if you're singing with your heart and allowing your heart to control. And if, when you're sitting on a stage, you're so into the song that you're not thinking about what note you're going to hit, it's like you're hallucinating, it's like you're dreaming!"[105]

Another hero for Buffy was Harry Belafonte. She loved his Caribbean island music and his skills as a performer, but what Buffy appreciated most was the way he helped other people. Belafonte always welcomed having Indigenous performers share the stage with him.

Buffy is an intellectual in her lyrics but purely a natural in her music. Because of her dyscalculia (music dyslexia), she composes by playing everything with multi-tracking tape recorders and computers. In her 1971 *Buffy Sainte-Marie Songbook*, Buffy describes the joys and challenges of her musical ability, which mysteriously seem to arise spontaneously. She feels that the music has always been there for her to listen to, and that she has been blessed with an "inner media" that brings her great joy and which makes the rest of life seem pale by comparison. For Buffy, it could be easy to ignore the rest of the world and only listen to the music playing in her head.

"What can I say about songwriting? I don't know anything about it. To ask me about songwriting is like asking a patient to talk about a disease he was born with. Songs are something in and of themselves. They come unbidden. Song stuff writes me—I don't write it. I discover a song already formed and playing in my head. Now and then I run into James Taylor or Carole King or Joni Mitchell or Bob Dylan or Mick Jagger, but so what? We never talk about songwriting, and as far as I can see, each of us lives in his own world.

"I write about what I hear in my head or what might have happened to a friend, or something I have heard about. That's what I mean by personal. Hearing a song in your head in the middle of the night is like trying to ignore a whale in your bathtub. You have to do something with it."[106]

Buffy does not shy away from courageously exploring the inner forces of musical creativity. She feels that, for a songwriter, songs come from their experience—the emptiness or fullness of what is going on in their life. That may be about being in love, having a broken heart, having to work hard, or having a bad case of the blues. She believes these emotions come from the same place as dreaming. Part of this place is reality and part of it is a mental, emotional, and spiritual processing. Buffy receives songs that blow her mind, that she perceives as spiritual songs. She will have something in mind and the lyrics will unfold from someplace that feels inspired. For her, songwriting can also be fun, like doing a puzzle. Then other times it takes inspiration and perspiration.[107]

One of Buffy's writing techniques is to keep a notebook in her purse. She scribbles idea fragments or lyrics in notebooks that she has kept over the years. She might think of something while walking down the grocery aisle or through an airport, perhaps a silly lyric or a blues riff or something else totally unique. When Buffy feels like composing, she sits down and reviews her notebooks. There may be something she wrote last week that matches something she wrote last year. Themes often appear again and again in different ways. She has written both protest and love songs this way.

Buffy can't say whether it's the music or the lyrics that come first to her. At best, they come together in what she describes as a kind of "helicopter vision." She may get an idea, akin to trying a new recipe. First, she "tastes" the whole thing in her mind. The ingredients then come from her life and what inspires her.

Buffy cannot say for sure that she knows what music is about. She believes it is probably a very high form of nonverbal communication. She has taught songwriting and believes a songwriter can teach people a lot. But she discourages people from trying to write songs just to meet a deadline. For her, songwriting has to be spontaneous and the content must already be inside her.

Regardless of technique, Buffy maintains that the ability to write songs cannot be forced. She feels sorry for kids whose parents make them take piano lessons. That can scare the creativity out of most children. She feels kids should be allowed to do what interests them. Performing music should be playful, not mechanical and just a job. "Chet Atkins told me that somebody asked if he reads music. His answer was 'not enough to hurt my playing!' That was perfect for me. Barbara Streisand, Celine Dion: these are virtuoso singers, perfect like violinists. Opera singers and classically-trained people can hit a note perfectly. That's different from what untrained natural musicians do. We do something else, also valuable, but not the same thing at all. I love to listen to a virtuoso, but it's not what I'm trying to do. I'm possessed by the song like falling in love and trying to have a good time, or at least survive within it. If I'm successful it's because I'm lucky ... for me the songs just happen as part of my life."[108]

Despite her "luck," Buffy realizes how elusive success can be. Contemplating her music career, she seems astounded by what she has accomplished. "You know, I didn't think I was going to last and the stakes weren't very high, so I was just going to be there for a while. I just said, 'Okay, go for it.' I was so shy that I couldn't even think about what I sounded like personally. It was all about the content of the song.

"The only way I had the courage to get on a stage was because I believed in the songs and what they said. I couldn't sound like somebody else, so why not just open up your heart and let it rip? I was a terrible singer, I think, on my first few records, but what people loved were the songs and the passion with which I sang them. And they could tell that they were true, and they really were!"[109]

Buffy didn't enter the music business thinking she would automatically have some kind of career. She had neither the music education nor the business background to understand music as a profession. In fact, Buffy sometimes thinks she got where she is by accident.

Who knows what tomorrow brings
In a world where few hearts survive
All I know is the way I feel
If it's real, I'll keep it alive
The road is long
And there are mountains in our way
But we climb a step everyday
"Up Where We Belong"

Musician Robbie Robertson, who is part-Mohawk, feels that Buffy occupies a special place as a songwriter. He calls her a "spiritual weaver" because of the way she uses her lyrics. He says she sings about beauty and how one should think positively, even in the face of negative things. Robertson believes that songs such as "Starwalker" can prove to be more powerful than a sword.[110]

Seasoned performer Randy Bachman observes that songs like "Universal Soldier" and "Up Where We Belong" were really written from the heart. He feels that, as a songwriter, if you can't find singers who can deliver your message, and if you believe strongly in that message, you end up having to become a performer yourself. He likes the way Buffy constantly experiments with each record and feels the most important and powerful ones were *Little Wheel Spin and Spin* and *Illuminations*, the groundbreaking, electronic album from 1969.[111]

Aboriginal singer/actor Tom Jackson also appreciates the wisdom of Buffy's approach. He calls her songwriting very honest, very poetic, and very musical. He feels that Buffy appreciates the old saying that one can attract more flies with honey than with vinegar. He also feels she is teaching the world and making it a better place by giving us information and commentary about subject matter that most people probably don't even want to talk about.[112]

Part of Buffy's talent as a musician and songwriter includes her ability to spot talent. She played a vital role in helping the career of Joni Mitchell. Born Joan Anderson, Mitchell grew up in Saskatoon, Saskatchewan, and started her career singing at various venues in that province.

Mitchell was drawn to the songwriters of her generation, including Buffy, Bob Dylan, and Leonard Cohen. She thought they were articulate and fresh. In 1964 she went east to see Buffy headline the Mariposa Folk Festival in Orillia, Ontario. Buffy played both the mouthbow and guitar at that performance, using D modal (also known as Celtic) tuning as opposed to the usual Spanish tuning. This influenced Mitchell's approach to guitar tuning and she began to experiment with her own instrument. Both singers had ties to Saskatchewan and they hit it off right away, becoming lifelong mutual admirers.

Liking her music, Buffy carried Mitchell's tape in her purse while she toured. Whenever it seemed right she would play it for music business people, trying to get Mitchell a record contract. Buffy also recorded several of Mitchell's songs. One song Buffy covered was Mitchell's "The Circle Game," its lyrics written in response to singer Neil Young's lament that he was growing too old to enjoy the fairgrounds. The song reassured listeners that "there'll be new dreams, maybe better dreams and plenty."

By 1964, Mitchell was playing the Toronto coffeehouse circuit but was still a struggling singer. She met folk singer Chuck Mitchell in 1965 and married him after a quick courtship. The couple moved to an apartment on Detroit's Wayne State University campus, where Eric Anderson, Buffy, Gordon Lightfoot, Tom Rush, and others would occasionally stop by. In 1966, seeking her own freedom and identity as an artist, Mitchell moved to New York City.

Buffy's manager at the time was Joel Dean of the Chartoff-Winkler agency. Dean didn't pick up on what Buffy perceived as Mitchell's tremendous potential as a singer and songwriter. The agency had just hired a young guy named Elliot Roberts. Mitchell was performing for $15 a night at New York's Café au Go Go when Buffy brought Roberts to see the show. While Roberts described Mitchell as a jumble of creative clutter with a guitar case full of napkins, road maps, and scraps of paper covered with lyrics, he was impressed enough that he became her manager. Roberts secured a long-term recording contract for Mitchell that allowed her to pursue singing as a professional career. Thus Buffy was instrumental in launching Mitchell's successful career.

At about the time Buffy was moving to Kauai in 1967, Mitchell was moving from New York to Laurel Canyon, outside of Los Angeles. Mitchell and James Taylor flew to Kauai to visit Buffy and Dewain Bugbee. On the way, stopping overnight in Honolulu,

Mitchell looked out a window and saw beautiful green mountains in the distance. She then looked down and saw a parking lot stretching as far as the eye could see—a blight on paradise. That scene motivated Mitchell to write the song "Big Yellow Taxi" with its lyrics, "They paved paradise and put up a parking lot."

The Woodstock Music Festival in August 1969 was organized by four young entrepreneurs to showcase counterculture music. The site originally planned was cancelled as local authorities feared the congregation of 50,000 stoned hippies. Finally, organizers managed to secure a piece of pastureland on a farm owned by Max Yasgur. Word of the event rapidly spread and, in the end, 500,000 youth descended on the site. This was far more than originally planned for, and the festival suffered from inadequate food and sanitation, and massive traffic jams, all compounded by heavy rain.

Music lovers were treated to Joan Baez, Joe Cocker, the Grateful Dead, Richie Havens, Jimi Hendrix, Jefferson Airplane, Janis Joplin, and many other performers. Despite the drawbacks, Woodstock was an overwhelmingly peaceful and happy festival. Yasgur later commented that if more people had joined the celebration, many of America's problems might have been solved. Albums and a movie of the event were highly profitable, and Woodstock became a cultural phenomenon.

Woodstock impressed Joni Mitchell as being a modern miracle—a modern-day fishes and loaves story. While Mitchell did not sing at Woodstock (appearing on *The Dick Cavett Show* instead at the insistence of her agent), she astutely penned her

Buffy with Leonard Cohen. Like Buffy, Cohen did not receive formal musical training and was an inspiration and source of moral support to her.

thoughts in the brilliant song "Woodstock." The song became the unofficial anthem of the iconic event and further propelled Mitchell into music fame. Mitchell would subsequently sign with highly successful record producer David Geffen at Asylum Records.

Woodstock might have been a prime event for Buffy, given her antiwar stance, but she was preoccupied with Native American issues not generally examined by the mainstream music scene. Interesting, Mitchell and Buffy are so iconic of that era, that even today people come up to both with comments about how good they were at Woodstock, even though neither appeared there.

Although essentially a loner, Buffy loved other contemporary artists and supported them, just as they supported her. Leonard Cohen's 1966 novel, *Beautiful Losers*, based on the story of the mysticism of Iroquois Catholic Saint Kateri Tekakwitha and her conversion to Catholicism, fascinated her. Buffy can't remember exactly how she met Cohen, but she admired *Beautiful Losers*. She came across this passage in the book: "god is alive, magic is afoot, god is alive, god is afoot, magic is alive" and loved it. Buffy decided to record the words and the result is her spontaneous recording "God is Alive, Magic is Afoot." Cohen has always loved her orchestration of his words.

"We both used to stay at the Chelsea Hotel in New York from time to time. And we became friends and I just always have had this immense respect for him. He was so humble; he used to say that he didn't know why he was a candidate to make a record; he didn't think he could sing. He used to say, 'I have a very human voice,' and that really is to me the basis of charm for any singer ... that's what he went with and that's what he gives us and that's what's wonderful."[113]

Cohen has been described as a brooding poet, novelist, romanticist, and songwriter. Like Buffy, he did not receive formal musical training and to her he was an inspiration and source of moral support. "He is obviously not a product of the CGD 7th school of songwriting ... Most songwriters use a very simple melodic line if the words are of great merit, and vice-versa, but not Leonard Cohen. He has the delicious gall to ask us, who do not even know him, to follow him into a completely original and sometimes scary mind of words without the aid of any of the old folksy musical clichés we are used to holding onto as a guide-rail ...

"Cohen's songs are both other-worldly and incredibly mortal, as I find Cohen himself to be ... He'll be called vague, aimless, or cloudy. But I, for one, am grateful to him for lifting me off the familiar musical ground. It's curious to start off in one key and then find yourself in another, and have no idea how you got there. It's like losing track of time ... "[114]

> *God never sickened;*
> *Many poor men lied*
> *Many sick men died*
> *Magic never weakened*
> *Magic never hid*
> *Magic always ruled*
> *God is afoot*
> *God never died.*

"God is Alive, Magic is Afoot," words by Leonard Cohen, set to music and sung by Buffy Sainte-Marie

In June 1972, at the height of her career, Buffy performed a one-woman show at the Dorothy Chandler Pavilion in Los Angeles. Buffy sang "Until It's Time for You to Go" as her finale, and the near-capacity audience refused to let her go, chanting to hear yet one more song.

As for the performance, Buffy says, "People ask if I am singing to 100,000 people, don't I get nervous? I say no, because I am singing to one person. I am singing that song to one person—it stays that intimate."[115] To Buffy, the songs are vital to the soul, to who you are, who you want to be, and who you can affect.

CHAPTER 7

SPEAKING OUT: THE SOCIAL ACTIVIST

Buffy tends to shy away from a description of herself as an activist, preferring to think of herself as a songwriter with information. While she did not make a conscious decision to focus on American Indian issues, it was obvious that Aboriginal needs were not well covered during the civil rights years. That was where Buffy felt she could make her main contribution. She could lend her fame, profile, and media access to the cause for fundraising and awareness. Buffy's goal was to be effective in bringing about social change, and songwriting was her obvious tool. Her paintings, speeches, and teaching messages were saturated with her trademark passion, often conveyed to small audiences in rural places where such problems were prominent but not discussed. Whether in fancy cities or in the middle of nowhere, her message sometimes included outrage, but was always accompanied by hope and strategy. In the 1980s, Buffy began to gear her message more toward children because she believed youth, too, have a chance to change the world.

The Vietnam War began almost imperceptibly in 1956 with a small number of American "advisors." By the early 1960s, this number expanded into small groups of "Special Operations Forces," conducting commando operations. Ultimately there was escalation to full-fledged offensive operations against North Vietnamese armed forces and Communist supporters (commonly known as the Viet Cong): the goal—to "defend" American interests in South Vietnam. By 1968, under President Lyndon Johnson, U.S. military personnel in Vietnam would peak at 536,100. Ironically, the U.S. had never made any official declaration of war. Vietnam was war by proxy, part of the Cold War, as superpowers China and Russia and the United States supported allies in North or South Vietnam. Most Americans weren't really certain why they were fighting, apart from the generally vague need to "halt the Communist threat."

Fighting in Vietnam occurred at close quarters in heavily forested jungle environments, resulting in high casualty rates. By the war's end in 1973, 58,226 American troops had been killed, and 153,303 wounded. These numbers paled beside the estimated 1,700,000 dead and wounded on the North Vietnamese side.

During this time, the concept of protest became part of America's mainstream vocabulary, and social activism broke out on the country's college and university campuses. Students carried the message that war was not the only, or even the best, way to solve the world's problems.

Popular Vietnam-era protest songs include Bob Dylan's

"Masters of War," John Lennon's "Give Peace a Chance," and Crosby, Stills, Nash and Young's "Ohio," (which mourned the four students killed by National Guardsmen at Kent State University in 1970). Country Joe McDonald's "I Feel Like I'm Fixin' to Die Rag" featured sarcastic lyrics like "Uncle Sam needs your help again, he's got himself in a terrible jam way down in Vietnam ... what are we fighting for? Don't ask me I don't give a damn." However, many feel that Buffy's "Universal Soldier," ("He's been a soldier for a thousand years ... he knows he shouldn't kill and he knows he always will") was the era's most intriguing song because it ended with a question and an open chord.

Buffy recalls that the idea of "Universal Soldier" came to her late one night in early 1963, in the San Francisco airport, waiting for a morning flight to Toronto. She was scheduled to perform at Yorkville's Purple Onion coffeehouse and folk den. Buffy knew the United States government was denying any involvement in the Vietnam conflict but she saw a bunch of soldiers come through the airport, some helping buddies on gurneys and in wheelchairs. Some of the men were wounded, some were unconscious, and all looked very, very weary. Later, Buffy found out they were part of the special operations forces quietly helping to fight Viet Cong insurgents. During the flight to Toronto, Buffy could not stop thinking about what she had seen. She began to work on the song that became "Universal Soldier."

Buffy had thought carefully about "Universal Soldier's" lyrics: "He's 5 foot 2 and he's 6 feet 4 ... he's a Catholic, a Hindu, an atheist, a Jain." Five-foot-two and six-foot-four were the minimum and maximum heights allowed for soldiers; seventeen to thirty-one were the age parameters. Jainism is an ancient religion of India that teaches that people should not kill any living thing. Each succinct word in the song holds weight and meaning.

Beverlie Robertson, a part-time singer who lived across the street from the Purple Onion, recalls seeing Buffy: "She was beginning to wow people wherever she went. The Onion housed performers at the Ford Hotel, across from the Greyhound bus station ... an awful place with peeling paint and shared bathrooms. I was appalled and immediately invited her to stay with me. [Buffy] was a lovely person and still is. She was working on a few songs, including 'Universal Soldier.' She asked me if people would know what a Jain is ... I assured her that, if they didn't, the context of the song would make it plain."[116]

Buffy's emotional reaction to the injustice of what she thought of as the "war racket" was strong, and she decided to use the song as a vehicle to speak out and to educate. Buffy was not acting on behalf of any particular group, although she stood out among the ranks of the small but increasing number of antiwar musicians who acted out of a sense of personal conviction, hoping that their music would lead to positive social change. This activism had risks and consequences.[117]

"Universal Soldier" automatically categorized me as somebody with something to say in a time when you weren't supposed to say anything. For instance, the United States government was saying there was no war in Vietnam and yet my song "Universal Soldier" was being picked up as an anthem for the 1960s peace movement. And this meant that I was definitely not going to be allowed to be played on certain radio stations or invited to certain television stations."[118]

"Universal Soldier" became known as the battle hymn of draft card burners. It also became the unofficial anthem of some Vietnam veterans. Soldiers' bunks reveal all manner of black-inked writings and drawings. Many soldiers simply record their names and ETS (Estimated Time of Separation). During the Vietnam War, however, many of these scribblings reflected the antiwar emotions of young men being sent to a place on the other side of Earth, knowing there was a real possibility they might be returning in a flag-draped box. "You're the one who gives his body as a weapon of the war and without you all this killing can't go on," inscribed one soldier on his bunk bed, borrowing lyrics from "Universal Soldier." John Kay, leader of the rock band Steppenwolf, called "Universal Soldier" a timeless message, one which spoke to those who resolved that they could not support the Vietnam War.

Buffy's message ran headlong against American policy, particularly after the military draft began in 1965. President Lyndon Johnson's efforts to pursue the war effort reached a fever pitch that year and Buffy's call for individual responsibility did not sit well with a government that was harshly critical of draft dodgers.

"I didn't know that I was taking risks. I didn't know any better. I assumed that in America you could say what you wanted to say.

A lot of people were doing it—speaking out—only we were doing it in a way that it seemed like loose cannon. We weren't doing it as political speeches for a political party. I thought the ideas could be effective in making change and entertaining at the same time. I always knew that. I always had that clearly in my mind.

"At first I thought, well, my concert audiences are full, I'm being played on the radio, amazing! I'm a singer! And then Kennedy was assassinated and Johnson took over and all of sudden my radio play stopped, my phone was tapped. I was no longer as welcome in America."[119]

Despite having written "Universal Soldier," Buffy avoided photo-ops and mass protest marches, preferring instead to focus on Native rights and environmental issues, where there were no stars, no cameras. She had been thinking deeply about her real cause, "And so I put my time into Indian rights and I think that this is something that I know something about and I think my time is best spent, so far as my political views are concerned."[120]

In the early 1960s, Buffy learned of a threat to the Seneca First Nation, whose tribal land is located in upstate New York. The Kinzua Dam, which would be one of the largest dams in the United States east of the Mississippi River, would flood one-third of the Seneca Reservation, including valuable agricultural lands.

The Seneca launched an ambitious publicity campaign against the project and even drew the sympathy of President John Kennedy. Part of the Seneca protest was based upon a treaty signed with General George Washington, wherein the Seneca declared allegiance to the fledgling United States. Washington pledged: "Your great object seems to be the security of your remaining lands, and I have therefore, upon this point, meant to be sufficiently strong and clear. That in the future you cannot be defrauded of your lands; that you possess the right to sell and the right of refusing to sell your lands."[121]

Buffy did not hesitate to speak. "A couple of years ago, the government unilaterally broke the oldest treaty in Congressional archives, which George Washington, the "father of America," had drawn up with the Seneca Indians of New York state, granting recognition that the Seneca reservation belonged to the Seneca now and forever more. But the treaty was broken by the government. Kinzua Dam was built on the reservation, although there were several alternative sites, and the Seneca were evicted."[122] In the end, the U.S. Supreme Court dismissed the Seneca concerns, stating that the general interests of the public took preference over the treaty. In the Seneca's view, their interests had been sacrificed for political and economic gain. Buffy's song "Now That the Buffalo's Gone" was an effort to spotlight the struggle the Seneca faced against business and government violation of their rights and land:

> *Has a change come about Uncle Sam?*
> *Or are you still taking our lands?*
> *A treaty forever George Washington signed*
> *Consider dear lady, consider dear man*
> *And the treaty's been broken by Kinzua Dam*

And what will you do for these ones?
"Now That the Buffalo's Gone"

Although many, including Buffy, considered the Kennedy era one of great hope, Buffy was well aware of political games and did not mince words in challenging authority when she was sure the administration was wrong. "Who were the best of the Kennedys? John, right? Well who built the Kinzua Dam? He did. Who is the chairman of the Senate committee on Indian education? Teddy. Who wasn't even going to show up at a conference he promised to attend, when thousands of Indian students came, until he had to be publically embarrassed on TV and then showed up? Teddy ... Politics is politics and Indian people have been exploited by all of them for too many years."[123]

In 1966, Buffy and Dick Gregory were invited to perform at a rally in Saskatoon, Saskatchewan, to try to save the sacred Cree monument Mistaseni, a 363-tonne (400-ton) glacial rock in the shape of a resting buffalo. The monument was threatened by flooding due to construction of the giant Gardiner Dam, one of the largest earth-fill dams in the world. An effort to rescue the stone from demolition failed, but a portion was retrieved and used for a commemorative site.

Later, Gregory visited the Piapot Reserve that Buffy called home: "Dick Gregory came to my reserve and he knows Black problems, he knows poverty, he's seen poverty, or he thought he had seen poverty. He thought he had seen problems with the government.

He thought he'd seen problems between white and non-white, but he left completely amazed, with his head blown off his shoulders. He cried on the plane and told me he'd had no idea that there was anybody lower than what he thought was the bottom."[124]

Gregory could see for himself that American Indian poverty was a blind spot in the American psyche. By the time she stood up for Mistaseni in 1966, it was becoming clearer in Buffy's mind where she stood as a social commentator and activist.

"The things that I'm concerned with aren't so much with Vietnam or civil rights, because they should be represented by people who know what's what. I haven't been brought up in a Negro slum. And although I think these things are important, I think they are getting enough attention. My goodness, if Joan Baez and Harry Belafonte and Sammy Davis, Jr. are all trying to call attention to a certain fact, I don't think my name is going to make that much difference. And so I put all my time into Indian rights."[125]

Much more controversial involvement awaited Buffy as the struggle for American Indian rights intensified. The American Indian Movement (AIM) first surfaced in Minneapolis in 1968 when the activist organization established the Minneapolis AIM Patrol to address issues of police brutality. Many Indians arrested for something or nothing at all were unaware of their civil rights and would simply give up and go to jail. Another impetus for the movement was the rectification of historical wrongs, such as broken treaties. AIM intended to use high-profile social and political action to confront injustices on the part of the state, as well as loss of cultural identity and corruption within Indian communities.

AIM's public visibility strategy was perfect for Buffy. She did a lot of concerts as fundraisers in the 1970s and was an important asset to the movement. Her greatest value was in raising public awareness among level-headed people. Buffy hoped that the American public, which seemed sympathetic to Native American rights, would react positively if they understood the facts. She had already demonstrated her faith in an informed American citizenry when, in 1969, she spoke out about a question regarding Native fishing rights in Washington State, appealing to citizens who would have been unaware of the situation. She knew from her own research that the Indians of Washington State had treaty rights to fish that were guaranteed by the United States government. But when the state began denying the Indians their right to fish, roughing them up and throwing them in jail, the federal government was nowhere to be seen. She felt that it was up to young Indian people to inform themselves about what was going on and get the word out to the public about these injustices. This is what Buffy stated she was trying to do—to be a kind of spokesperson each time she appeared on television, radio, or the concert circuit.[126]

AIM believed that radical action was necessary to produce real change, although Buffy preferred to appeal to the masses via the media. She thought of her approach as feminine, the other side of the masculine approach of the AIM founders. Buffy also worked with the AIM movement to turn its attention toward respecting women and elders, and renewing Indian spirituality, which would then provide the needed strength to ripen immature and destructive American political policies.

In 1969, activists in the San Francisco Bay area sought to reclaim abandoned Alcatraz Island under the Fort Laramie Treaty of 1868, which included a stipulation that surplus federal land was to be returned to American Indians. Their claim was not taken seriously and seemed to become irrelevant when rumours spread that wealthy developer Lamar Hunt wanted to build a casino on the island. An American Indian student group, based out of the University of California, Berkeley, and San Francisco State University, developed an action plan in response. On the evening of November 14, 1969, a group of students hired a fishing boat to drop them off on Alcatraz, which was officially closed to the public. Within days, word of the occupation spread and dozens more protestors joined the group. The story made national and international headlines.

The U.S. Coast Guard swung into action to prevent any further individuals, supplies, or water barges from reaching Alcatraz. The protestors were forced to hatch plans to divert the Coast Guard's attention. These schemes involved shooting ineffective homemade arrows at Coast Guard boats, staging a boat "collision," and having an occupier fall into San Francisco Bay (fortunately, the Coast Guard rescued that person before he was swept too far away in the frigid waters). While these diversions took place, Alcatraz occupants busily unloaded supplies on the other side of the island. In one 1970 interview, Buffy recalled what happened when the power to the island was terminated: "They cut off the electricity, which also powered a lighthouse, even though there were ships in the water. So we had to power the generator by hand to help the boats out of the water. The boat owners were so thankful that they started carrying the press out to the island from the mainland. But all those ship captains who helped us found out later that their licences had been cancelled and insurance companies were revoking their coverage. That's why no one heard anything about Alcatraz."[127]

John Trudell, a Santee Sioux who set up Radio Free Alcatraz, kept Buffy informed of events and encouraged her to join the many First Nations groups who were pitching in to do what they could. Buffy lent her voice in support of the occupation and used her concert money to buy water for the Alcatraz occupiers.

A local inter-university Native student group arranged for a series of benefit concerts to raise money and bring visibility. Buffy played at Memorial Church on the Stanford University campus at one of the first events on December 18, 1969. Student Shirley Keith kicked off the evening with a lengthy explanation of American Indian grievances and land claims, but her speech seemed to go over most peoples' heads until parallels were drawn to the conflict in Vietnam. The opening musical act was Malvina Reynolds, who sang a special composition praising Native spirituality and condemning Lamar Hunt's plans for a casino on the island.

Then the audience heard Buffy's performance. Her songs

"Now That the Buffalo's Gone" and "My Country 'Tis of Thy People You're Dying" cut right to the heart of the issues and were received enthusiastically. Richard Oakes, initiator of the Alcatraz occupation, came onstage to present Buffy with a bouquet of flowers and read the Alcatraz Proclamation: "We the Native Americans, reclaim the land known as Alcatraz Island in the name of all American Indians by right of discovery. We wish to be fair and honorable in our dealings with Caucasian inhabitants of this land, and hereby offer the following treaty: We will purchase said Alcatraz Island for twenty-four dollars in glass beads and red cloth, a precedent set by the white man's purchase of a similar island [Manhattan] about 300 years ago ..."[128]

The proclamation added plans to establish a Center of Native American Studies on the island. Trudell emerged as the most articulate spokesman for Alcatraz. He would later become national chairman of AIM and one of Buffy's most respected friends during her years of activism.

Despite the passion and forthrightness of the Alcatraz occupation, government intimidation and internal division caused the protest to fall apart in the summer of 1971, after nineteen months and the participation of 5,600 people. Nevertheless, the protest would have a profound effect on the lives of Native Americans as it became a prominent symbol of the radical political movement embodied by the American Indian Movement.

In 1972, AIM organized the Trail of Broken Treaties march to Washington, D.C. President Richard Nixon's administration was proposing a new Indian policy called "self-determination." American Indian leaders believed the policy would be another attempt to strip them of their rights and land. A twenty-point manifesto was presented to Nixon, demanding a review of Indian treaties, restitution for violations, and the creation of new treaty and administrative relations with American Indians.

Buffy, like other Indian activists, was openly critical of Indian policy, but such outspokenness could come at a price. It was later revealed that the FBI had used invented information to keep civil rights and antiwar activists under surveillance or subject them to covert attempts to suppress their voice, sometimes permanently. Following the Alcatraz occupation, FBI activities were soon directed against AIM. There was evidence that the agency had been actively infiltrating AIM.

In February 1973, AIM was contacted by Lakota elders for assistance in dealing with corruption within the Bureau of Indian Affairs and the Tribal Council at the Pine Ridge Reservation in South Dakota. The Pine Ridge Reservation, one of the poorest enclaves in the nation, had long been plagued by varying degrees of turmoil. The tribal government, considered by many to be paid-off puppets of the Bureau, allowed large corporations access to the reservation for strip mining, activities that defaced the earth and the environment, and provided little benefit to the Indians. Expecting trouble from AIM, the tribal administration called in law enforcement.

AIM and its supporters made their stand at the hamlet of

Wounded Knee, coincidentally the site of the 1890 massacre of the same name. As events unfolded, hundreds of U.S. Marshalls, Bureau of Indian Affairs police, FBI agents, and military personnel arrived, bringing with them heavy-caliber machine guns, armoured personnel carriers, and helicopters. The government's strategy was to surround the occupiers and starve them into submission but this failed when food was smuggled in. During the nearly three-month occupation at Wounded Knee, the U.S. National Guard and Wounded Knee protestors exchanged sporadic gunfire, resulting in the deaths of two Indian men, Buddy Lamont and Frank Clearwater. As the army surrounded Wounded Knee with tanks and soldiers, the violence made international headlines.

On March 25, 1973, Buffy performed at a mass at New York's Cathedral of St. John the Divine in support of the occupation. Nearly 4,000 people attended, including Reverend Vine Deloria, Sr., who delivered the sermon. "May your cause be heard by all the people in America," he said before listing the sad facts that the government was "forcing Native Americans to accept [white] culture ... violating their gravesites ... destroying their lands with the mining industry ... [entertaining Indians] by movies celebrating their genocide."[129] Just days earlier, Marlon Brando had refused to accept an Academy Award for his performance in *The Godfather* (in his stead, Brando sent Apache activist Sacheen Littlefeather to read a statement condemning Wounded Knee and Hollywood's misrepresentation of American Indians), opting to be at Wounded Knee instead. The media blitz and efforts by performers like Buffy and Brando had an effect. Ninety-three percent of Americans were following the story and a majority supported the Wounded Knee protestors.

Finally, on May 5, 1973, after seventy-two days, protestors and government officials reached an agreement allowing the occupiers to disarm and the authorities to assume control of Wounded Knee. But the violence was hardly over. On June 26, 1975, Joe Stuntz, another Native American man, and two FBI agents died in a shootout between the FBI and Bureau of Indian Affairs police, also at the Pine Ridge Reservation. Indian activists, including Leonard Peltier, were arrested and subjected to a prolonged ordeal involving falsified documents, illegal extradition from Canada, and a trial full of anti-AIM bias. Peltier remains in jail to this day.

Buffy began to devote even more time to performing benefit concerts and getting out the message that the public needed to address Aboriginal grievances. Her efforts to change peoples' attitudes went through phases. In the 1960s, while still in her twenties, Buffy was concerned with educating the general public: "The Bureau of Indian Affairs in the United States was not set up to protect us as some people believe, but rather to take care of the government's problem of how to get rid of Indians and exploit the land ... If there's one single thing I'm trying to do for Indians as a composer, it's to inform the white community and explain the way things really were ... I think that people need to be informed if they're going to do the right thing by the Indians."[130]

Now that the longhouses breed superstition
You force us to send our toddlers away
To your schools where they're taught to despise their traditions
You forbid them their languages, then further say
That American history really began
When Columbus set sail out of Europe, then stress
That the nation of leeches that conquered this land
Are the biggest and bravest and boldest and best.
And yet where in your history books is the tale
Of the genocide basic to this country's birth,
Of the preachers who lied, how the Bill of Rights failed
How a nation of patriots returned to their earth
"My Country 'Tis of Thy People You're Dying"

In 1972 Buffy said, hopefully, "A new kind of American is emerging. People are coming around, catching on. It seems to me people are becoming more open to new ideas and to each other. I find people reaching out to each other, helping each other a little more, not being so pushy." However, Buffy was also realistic. "It's a do-it-yourself world. I'm not going to wait for anybody to help me. I've waited ten years. I sang 'Now That the Buffalo's Gone' until I was sick of people coming to see the little Indian girl cry. But nothing happened, did it? The change is going to have to come from within us, the Indian people."[131]

During her years of involvement with many American and Canadian Aboriginal rights initiatives, Buffy watched a real movement take shape and she began to focus more on strategies to build up Indian self-awareness at the grass roots level through individuals and communities, as opposed to looking to nationally prominent Indian leadership. What was needed, Buffy concluded, was to build native self-esteem by focusing on the beauty and resilience of Indian culture. There needed to be a spotlight on the joy and celebration of Indian progress. Buffy began bringing high-energy rock and roll shows to the reservations. "I wanted to bring Indians up, not White people down."

Floyd "Red Crow" Westerman, a songwriter and one of AIM's most ardent supporters, recalled why he became an activist. "I grew up in boarding school. What that experience did to us was, the government wanted to assimilate Indians, in their words save the Indian, kill their soul. They teach the English language, assimilate them and then relocate them. In the end it was exterminate the culture, exterminate them. If all the Indians run to the city, they can take our land, and finally that would be the end of it."[132]

Westerman described the effect Buffy had on his life and outlook. Many of her songs had inspired him to realize that the voice of the Indian people had been muted for too long. Buffy provided the first example of how one could express native feelings about issues of land, culture, and spirituality. Westerman realized that the song lyrics had real power. "To get a voice onto the popular radio airwaves and have songs sung that speak about a point of view, about 'now that the buffalo is gone, what will you do my friend, what will you do for these ones?' was great. But they censored her songs at radio stations. So I think that makes Buffy the warrior of an unusual kind and especially being a woman. . .

"We went into Washington, D.C., and Buffy was there. We did a huge concert. The press followed us right out to the middle of the country, Kansas and places like that, the newspapers were writing about us all the way. The bill didn't pass [Congress], that's what it accomplished. We still have our treaties as a mainstay of talking to the government. Abrogation is now just a word that we'll never let slip by us. We know now we can control some things that happen."[133]

Westerman recalled Buffy's concern about Native children: "One of the first times that I did a concert with Buffy was for the American Indian Movement survival schools, held at the University of Minnesota. Harry Belafonte was there. Buffy's first priority was the children. She always wanted to work with schools in that educational kind of way. You could tell right away that her concern was for future generations."[134]

Buffy pulled together concerts, sometimes referred to as "medicine shows" to help heal native communities. Other stars like Willie Dunn, Charlie Hill, Shannon Two Feathers, and Floyd Westerman joined in. She wrote and sang songs like "He's an Indian Cowboy in the Rodeo," "Moonshot," "Native North American Child," and "Starwalker," partly with the medicine shows in mind. "Starwalker" came to be the American Indian Movement's unofficial anthem. Some of Buffy's fans feared that, by focusing on the American Indian audience, largely located on poverty-stricken reservations, Buffy was giving up a lucrative career in mainstream pop music. Moreover, she often irked her managers by donating the entire proceeds from a concert to some grassroots fund. Buffy was tenacious. "It seems like 90 percent of my time is spent in court or with the press, trying to explain and remedy the dire problems which cause the Indian suicide rate to be the highest in the country, infant mortality, unemployment, and poverty to be ten- and twenty-times anybody else's.

"I am one of many who are in this to the death. We stay up day and night for five, six, seven days in a row, flying to and from areas where our people face emergencies, emergencies which are preventable and which are often the direct result of illegal action on the part of the United States and Canadian governments and which are to the shame and disgrace of the North American people.[135]

Republican Richard Nixon became President in 1969 and held office until his resignation in 1974. While the Johnson administration saw Buffy as a loose cannon because of her effective stance against the Vietnam War, the Nixon administration was concerned about her ability to put the international spotlight on injustices against American Indians. Buffy was critical of Nixon's trying to portray himself as a friend of the Indian: "Most white Americans reading what Nixon is doing for the Indians think, 'Oh isn't that nice, this nice man is going to take care of it.' Then they forget about it … All I can say is that for years politicians have been putting on war bonnets and shaking rattles for twenty minutes out of their lives. I want somebody to show me what a politician has done. I am not interested in their promises anymore."[136]

In early 1975, Buffy participated in a benefit concert in St. Paul, Minnesota, supporting AIM survival schools—the Red Schoolhouse in St. Paul, the Heart of the Earth School in Minneapolis, and the We Will Remember School in Rapid City. Her fellow performers included Harry Belafonte, Rita Coolidge, and Kris Kristofferson. Buffy's friend Anna Mae Aquash was one of the most enthusiastic organizers.

Aquash, a young Micmac woman originally from Nova Scotia, came to Pine Ridge in 1973 at the age of twenty-three to support the American Indian Movement. Buffy met Aquash, was impressed by her intelligence and earnestness, and they became friends. Three years later, shockingly, Aquash's body was discovered at the bottom of a ravine near a desolate reservation highway on the edge of the South Dakota Badlands. An initial autopsy concluded that she had perished from exposure. However, after pressure from the Aquash family to exhume the body, a bullet was discovered in the back of her neck. Speculation quickly rose that she had been executed. Buffy would later pen "Bury My Heart at Wounded Knee" in her memory.

My girlfriend Annie Mae talked about uranium
Her head was filled with bullets and her body dumped
The FBI cut off her hands and told us she'd died of exposure
"Bury My Heart at Wounded Knee"

AIM activist Floyd Westerman recalled how in 1977 Buffy helped instigate another national march. "I happened to be in San Francisco and Buffy was in town. We were sitting around— Dennis Banks and me and Buffy. There was only the three of us in the room. We were talking about the bills that were about to be passed by the United States Congress to abrogate these treaties, and we figured that it was the most damaging kind of action that the government could take.

"Buffy insisted that we had to do something about it. And Dennis, who was really good at organizing youth, suggested the idea of bringing attention to these treaties by walking across the country. So began one of the most effective tools we could use, which was to march across America."[137]

In February 1978, a group of about 200 American Indian activists, led by Dennis Banks, left San Francisco on a 4828 km (3,000 mi.), six-month trek called the Longest Walk that would end at the Washington Monument in the national capital in July. Its purpose was to publicize grievances and protest proposed congressional legislation that threatened to terminate Indian treaties and break up the reservations. The march was launched at a press conference, with Buffy at Banks's side. Banks, who was wanted in South Dakota on a weapons charge, could not go outside the California border— Governor Jerry Brown had protected him from extradition.

Along the route, marchers were banned from some towns and faced the occasional media blackout. Other communities opened their homes or gave food, money, and clothing. The march culminated in a week of well-publicized workshops attended by several thousand people. A baby born at the end of the march was named Long Walker.

Sheldon Peters Wolfchild, who is the father of Buffy's son Cody, helped the walk by bringing in celebrities to put on benefits to raise funds. World-champion boxers Muhammad Ali and Ken Norton staged a twelve-round exhibition bout. Performing artists included Buffy, composer David Amram, actor Max Gail (*Barney Miller*), Floyd Westerman, Richie Havens, and Stevie Wonder. Brando was working on an ABC series he likened to an American Indian version of *Roots*, the epic dramatization of Black history. Buffy was seen showing Stevie Wonder how to play the mouthbow. Buffy also invited her nieces from Saskatchewan, Debbie Piapot and Marlyn Obey, to participate in the march and the two were thrilled to meet the people behind the famous names.

Several forceful speakers articulated the purpose behind the Longest Walk. These included Vern Bellecourt, a fiery AIM founder; Dick Gregory, who admonished the marchers about understanding their power; Representative Ron Dellems (Democrat–California), who gave a rousing speech about the need for humanism; and Marlon Brando, who on the steps of Congress, lamented that the United States lagged in human rights and was the last country to give up colonial control. Brando declared that Americans had much to learn from American Indians and their ability to live in harmony with nature. In the end, the Longest Walk was successful in scuttling the threatening legislation.

John Trudell was national chairman of the American Indian Movement from 1974 to 1980, a Vietnam veteran, and a close friend of Anna Mae Aquash. The FBI had amassed some 17,000 pages on Trudell's activities from 1969 to 1979. They described him as an intelligent, eloquent speaker with the ability to motivate people into action. They believed Trudell to be a known hardliner who openly encouraged the use of violence. It was claimed that he had the ability to meet with a group of pacifists and in a short time have them yelling and screaming, "right on!"[138]

John led the Longest Walk into Washington, D.C. while receiving veiled warnings that there would be retaliation if he continued to speak out. Nevertheless, he delivered a speech on the steps of the FBI building. Less than twelve hours later, on February 12, 1978, a fire tore through his family home on the Shoshone–Paiute Reservation in Nevada. John's wife, Tina, and their three children, all under five years old, were killed. Although the cause of the fire was never fully determined, to this day Trudell's supporters are certain it was set deliberately. It took many years for Trudell to recover from this trauma, but ultimately he did, and discovered the ability to use music as an outlet.

While Buffy worked hard to change public perceptions, inspire Native communities, and encourage educational opportunities, she did not realize her work was being undermined by the politics of two presidential administrations. Buffy's music began to disappear from the mainstream American airwaves during the 1970s, as

Lyndon Johnson assumed the U.S. presidency. Buffy thought that the decline of her record sales was just part of legitimate changes in American public taste. In reality, Buffy's record company was sending boxes of her recordings—which were actually very much in demand—to distributors; however, somewhere along the line, the boxes would simply disappear.

The Johnson White House had created a blacklist of performers whose music "deserved to be suppressed"—it included Buffy, Eartha Kitt, and Taj Mahal. Their personal convictions, like the lyrics to "Universal Soldier," were determined to encourage widespread citizen protest.

Johnson's campaign was continued by Richard Nixon. Broadcasters were flattered by letters from a presidential administration, feared not following White House directives, and may also have believed federal warnings about the potential dangers of these folk song "subversives." Increasingly, from around 1965 to 1975, Buffy's songs and albums experienced a serious lack of airplay as Buffy went from hit list to blacklist.

"After a certain point in the late '60s and into the '70s, I was doing concerts all over the world. When I'd come back to the United States, I'd have a full house. Everybody wanted to see me and they'd ask: We can't find your records—where can we buy them? I would get mad at Vanguard, thinking that they hadn't been shipping, but they said that they had been. It wasn't until the 1980s when I was doing a radio interview that I got a clue from a radio interviewer. He surprised me. He apologized to me for having been part of the campaign to suppress my music. He had a letter on White House stationery commending him for suppressing this music which deserved to be suppressed.'

"The part that hurt was really that we had been denied an audience in the U.S. I still had huge audiences in Asia and Down Under and Canada and Europe, but you couldn't even get my records all of a sudden. And if I were invited to come on to *The Tonight Show*, which I was, it was under the stipulation that I did not talk about Native rights or pacifism. So I said, no."[139]

Regardless of the pressure she was feeling at the time, Buffy continued to speak out. She gave benefit concerts to explain the position of political prisoner Leonard Peltier, who was serving two life terms in Leavenworth Prison (his parole was denied in 2009). Peltier was accused of playing a role in the deaths of the two FBI agents at Pine Ridge, but his supporters maintain that he was framed. On February 6, 1976, Peltier was captured by the Royal Canadian Mounted Police at a friend's cabin near Hinton, Alberta. He was subsequently convicted of the deaths of the two FBI agents, and the struggle to free him since has become an international cause célèbre.

We got the federal marshals, we got the covert spies
We got the liars by the fire and we got the FBI's
They lie in court and get nailed and still Peltier goes off to jail.
The bullets didn't match the gun!
"Bury My Heart at Wounded Knee"

Buffy began to sense that life for an American Indian activist could be very dangerous. It wasn't until years later that she was astonished to learn that the FBI had thirty-one pages of information on her in a secret file. In a 1999 suit against the United States government, ex-CIA agent Charles Schlund III revealed in court what he knew about the government's music blacklists. During his testimony, Schlund specifically stated that he supported Buffy's assertions that the United States took action to suppress rock music because of its role in rallying opposition to the Vietnam War. As late as 2009, Buffy was shocked to discover that the CIA, responsible for investigating international matters, was monitoring her as well.

The politically motivated censorship of antiwar music through two presidential administrations, one Democratic and one Republican, was effective. "It was hard seeing people hurt ... All that happened to me was that I was put out of business in the U.S., which is nothing in comparison to what happened to others. John Trudell had his family killed, his whole life put out of business. Joe Stuntz, Buddy Lamont, Frank Clearwater, Anna Mae Aquash, and even Leonard Peltier, though he lived, were put out of the living business—some were killed, and the rest of us were made less effective."[140]

The traumatic death of Annie Mae Aquash and the heated emotions surrounding Wounded Knee weighed heavily on Buffy's mind. Then her son Cody came into Buffy's life and this moved her to seriously contemplate taking a break from recording.

CHAPTER 8

MOTHERHOOD, ACTING, AND ART

＊

Buffy left Nashville for Los Angeles in 1975 to spend a week hosting a local morning entertainment news show. One evening, at an event hosted by the Los Angeles American Indian Center, she ran into her friend Ernie Peters, a Lakota of the Mdewakanton Sioux tribe in Minnesota and fellow activist during the early tumultuous AIM years. Peters introduced Buffy to his brother, Sheldon, a graduate of the prestigious Institute for American Indian Arts in Santa Fe, New Mexico. Sheldon was working in art props at Walt Disney Studios, had served in Vietnam, was a budding actor, and an American Indian activist. Floyd Westerman remembered Sheldon as someone who seemed like a quiet person when you first met him, but deep down was not really like that at all. Sheldon was committed to the American Indian Movement and recognized as having an influence in its direction.

Buffy was attracted to Sheldon and, in 1975, they married. The next summer their son, and Buffy's only child, Dakota (Cody) Starblanket Wolfchild, was born. Sheldon had not yet received

Emile, Buffy, Cody, Sheldon and others on the Piapot Reserve.

his traditional Indian name, so in 1976, during a visit to Buffy's Cree relatives at Rocky Boy's Reservation in Box Elder, Montana, Buffy's uncle, Henry Wolfchild, adopted the couple into his family. Sheldon Peters became Sheldon Peters Wolfchild and the family used the name Wolfchild from that time on.

Dakota means "ally" or "friend" in Sioux, and the child's middle name, Starblanket, which honours Buffy's maternal grandfather, Chief Starblanket, was used with her mother Clara's permission. Buffy calls Dakota "a wonder." Buffy's album *Sweet America* was released the year Cody was born. Although she had issued fourteen albums, Buffy rarely heard any of her songs on the radio. She thus began a sixteen-year semi-hiatus from concerts. She was disillusioned with the politics that seemed to be affecting the American scene and wanted to focus on being a mom. Buffy's creative life switched to home activities.

After Buffy's emergence into the limelight during the 1960s, she had consistently received offers from Hollywood to play this or that token Indian in movies that held no interest for her. "The problem was, and continues to be, that there are very few parts for Native American actors. The stories are always written by showbiz professionals, people who simply lack experience and knowledge of Native American communities, cultures, uniqueness, so the guts of the stories lack both charm and authenticity. The television series, *The Sopranos*, was wonderful because almost everybody involved— writers, directors, actors and all—had first-hand experience with the unique cultural background of the stories they were telling so it looks effortless and rich and real. Indian movies are typically created by outsiders and look phony. Who wants to be a part of that?"[141]

That said, Buffy had begun a promising Hollywood career in 1968 with her work on an episode of *The Virginian: The Heritage*, in which she played the role of Nai'Be. Jay Silverheels, a Mohawk Indian from the Six Nations Reserve in Ontario, who played Tonto in *The Lone Ranger*, was in the same episode. Buffy recalled Silverheels as the beautiful person who had started the Indian Actors Workshop. Buffy had met his aunt and uncle on the Six Nations Reserve and knew he was for real. Although there were many Indian roles in "cowboy and Indian" movies, most of the

Indians were played by painted-up white actors. Buffy strongly believed that the Indian roles, such as they were, should at least be played by Native American actors, and Silverheels's Indian Actors Workshop was developing these artists.

When asked by director Leo Penn, father of actor Sean Penn, to guest star on *The Virginian*, Buffy surprised him by telling producers that she "was not interested in playing Pocahontas" and insisted that the studio cast "real Indians" to play Native American roles. "No Indians, no Buffy." Penn and producer Joel Rogosin, she recalled, were "really great" about it, and she and Jay Silverheels quickly helped identify thirty prospective Native actors. At this time, Buffy's action was revolutionary and she was a leader in promoting authenticity and support for fellow Aboriginal artists. Twenty years later, when producers like Kevin Costner created films like *Dances with Wolves* and documentaries like *500 Nations*, the use of Aboriginal actors had come to be accepted.

In 1969 Buffy played the role of Tender Grass in *Then Came Bronson*, a short-lived NBC series about a newspaperman who sets out to travel America in search of the meaning of life. Eddie Little Sky, Lois Red Elk, and many other Indian actors got work on that series because of Buffy's lead. Buffy checked out but turned down parts in *McKenna's Gold* (1969) and *The Outlaw Josey Wales* (1976).

Charlie Hill is one of Buffy's closest friends. He is the only Native American stand-up comedian to appear on three major late-night talk shows: *Johnny Carson*, *David Letterman*, and *Jay Leno*. He has appeared in films alongside Robin Williams and Jim

Buffy (dismounting a horse in this shot from *The Virginian*) strongly believed that Indian roles on screen should at least be played by Native American actors.

Carrey, and was a writer for the show *Roseanne*. Hill's approach is to use irreverent humour to skewer racism and bridge cultural barriers. He tries to get people to laugh with Native Americans, rather than at them. Hill credits activists like Buffy for opening the doors for American Indian professional performers. He discovered that Buffy herself had something of a comedic talent when he convinced her to do some comedy skits.

"We did a television show once in Canada called *Indian Time* (1989). It was a sketch called 'Malcolm and Maisie' ... about a Cree couple and, when we started filming it, she had these hair rollers on, she started chewing gum, and she started doing this reservation accent that I'd never heard her do before. She just morphed into this person and I was amazed. I always thought if she wanted to she would have been a great comic actress."[142]

Recalling the same period, another of Buffy's friends, television producer and songwriter Curtis Jonnie, better known as Shingoose, recognized that Buffy was a natural when he saw her perform on *Indian Time*. "It was so good because it was kind of a takeoff on *The Honeymooners*. The first time that Buffy agreed to do the acting I guess it posed a challenge. And she just rose to it and completely nailed the character. It was so funny."[143]

Hill recalls first meeting Buffy in 1975—she quickly became one of the most important influences in his life. One of the things she taught him was that when he was on stage, he was the boss. That was all Hill needed to hear. Many of the things that Buffy was saying in her songs aligned with what Hill was saying in his comedy. She gave him the confidence to persevere and he is grateful to her for that.[144]

Shingoose remembers being overwhelmed when he first saw Buffy perform at Toronto's Massey Hall in 1974. There were not very many Aboriginal performers back then, other than Willie Dunn, Floyd Westerman, and a few others. Shingoose was backstage with some big stars like Gordon Lightfoot. Then Buffy came in. She ignored the big stars and walked right over to Shingoose and gave him a hug. He thought it was a message to the big stars that lesser-known Aboriginal performers were important, too.[145]

Shingoose was impressed by how "down to earth" Buffy was. "She's so attentive to you. If you are talking to her she's right there with you. There could be all kinds of stuff going on around you but she's right focused in on what you are saying. That's the sign of a true communicator. After you interact with her for a while, it's just like talking to your brother, your sister. You're just talking to another human being. The "star thing" is gone. She doesn't act like a snob or a star. She's not one of those people.[146]

"I remember one time being with Shingoose and we were at Max Gail's house. Max used to play Wojo in *Barney Miller*. So we had a production meeting for something, and Buffy had to get back to this college. I said, 'I'll give you a ride.' I had this old beat-up Volkswagen and she was wearing this John Travolta white outfit—it was just beautiful. She gets into the car and it just stinks! I had forgotten that it kept breaking down and burning oil. Finally we get about ten miles from where she's going and she made me stop the car. She gave me 100 bucks to fix it. I told her, 'You don't need a cab,' and we just kept going and breaking down. I didn't know until years later that she told my wife how greasy her outfit got!"[147]

Shingoose confirms Hill's recollection. They laughed a lot about it and Hill used it for one of his comedy routines. Here were people who professed to respect Mother Earth, and yet there they were in this Beetle with billowing smoke coming out.[148]

Despite all of her contacts in the film and television industry, Buffy's most high-profile opportunity to perform on mainstream media would come from an unexpected source and at just the right time.

The New York-based television show *Sesame Street* began in 1969 as a means of teaching social lessons to inner-city kids. Jim Henson's Muppets—Ernie and Bert, Cookie Monster, Big Bird, Oscar the Grouch, Kermit the Frog, and many others—interacted with human actors so the kids in the audience could learn the value of a specific letter, the intricacies of a number, or a social lesson. Thousands of viewers still recall the *Sesame Street* theme (Sunny day/Sweepin' the clouds away) that preceded each episode.

Sesame Street first aired on National Educational Television and later on PBS. It has received unprecedented international exposure, broadcasting three times each day in 120 countries and reaching millions of children. The longest-running children's series ever, *Sesame Street* has been nominated for 14 primetime and 253 daytime Emmys, winning 7 and 108 respectively. In 2009, the show was recognized with a Lifetime Achievement Emmy. Hundreds of celebrities and even world leaders have appeared on *Sesame Street*, from Kofi Annan and Bill Clinton to Ray Charles, Johnny Cash, and Michael Jackson to Julia Roberts and Adam Sandler.

One Nielsen Media Research survey revealed that 99 percent of American preschoolers could recognize a *Sesame Street* character. Muppets Bert and Ernie were oddly matched roommates who shared a basement suite on *Sesame Street*. Big Bird was an 8-foot,

2-inch (2.5-metre) yellow bird who resided in a large nest on an empty lot on *Sesame Street*, and was often visited by his friend Aloysius Snuffleupagus, a large, brown, woolly, elephant-like creature. Kermit the Frog tried to mediate the antics of the other *Sesame Street* characters. Count von Count loved counting on the show's Number of the Day segment, looking for a mystery number. Cookie Monster helped teach the Letter of the Day, but could never refrain from finally eating the letters.

Buffy remembers: "*Sesame Street* contacted me and asked me did I want to come on and do the alphabet and count from one to ten like Stevie Wonder and Burt Lancaster and everybody, and I said, 'No, not really.' And I said, however, 'Have you ever done any Native American programming,' and they said, 'No, but we'd like to.' For our first show we went to Taos Pueblo and we had a truck full of local kids. There were some Hopi kids and some Navajo kids, too, and Big Bird, and me. This was about 1975, before Dakota was born, and the way that this script was written—*Sesame Street* was so charming—Big Bird said, 'Buffy, I'm kind of nervous', and I said, 'Well, what is it, Big Bird?' And he said, 'I heard there were *Indians* around here.' And of course all the little kids popped up and said, 'Oh, Big Bird, you know, I'm Hopi and I'm Navajo,' and Big Bird felt better then. [The people behind *Sesame Street*] have my undying respect. I just think they're wonderful, the way they approach things—what a precious way to approach stereotyping before it ever hits. I learned a lot from them as a teacher and a person."[149]

Buffy had barely begun appearing on the show when she

learned that she and Sheldon were expecting a baby. Buffy told the producers, believing she would not be able to continue with the program, and was surprised when the producers said they would like to explore having a family on the show. This was a very appealing offer that fell in line with parenthood and her goals for educating the public. Buffy became a semi-regular cast member, appearing as herself from 1976 to 1981.

One of Buffy's primary motives for appearing on *Sesame Street* was the basic message: Indians *exist*. Buffy could often be heard greeting other characters with the traditional Cree greeting, *tansi*, and telling them that "We're not all dead and stuffed in museums." Episodes included "Buffy Nurses Cody," "Buffy Sings to Cody," "Cripple Creek," "Different People, Different Ways," "Wynken, Blynken and Nod," "The Count Counts in Cree," and "I'm Gonna be a Country Girl Again." One time Buffy even brought the cast to her own backyard in Hawaii for three weeks of multicultural shooting.

"I just had one goal; I just wanted little kids and their grown-ups to understand that Indians exist ... We are real, we have friends, we have family, we have music, we have culture, and we have a lot of fun. And it's that kind of message that you can make through a *Sesame Street*-kind of wondrous vehicle because it's so direct it cuts right through all the bureaucracy of education, politics, newspapers, publicity, it cuts through all of that and gets to the point: we are real."[150]

Buffy often praises the fact that *Sesame Street* never tried to stereotype her ethnicity. The producers were open to her suggestions

Buffy and Big Bird on *Sesame Street*

and she had a unique opportunity to explore several innovative educational topics, including sibling rivalry, multiculturalism, and breastfeeding. Buffy may well have been the first woman to breastfeed her child on national television.

"Big Bird represents the four-year-old in the audience, and one of the most beautiful things they did was the way they handled the topic of breast-feeding ... Little baby Dakota was nursing for real; I was sitting beside Big Bird's nest and Big Bird came by and he looked over my shoulder and said, 'Buffy, what're you doing?' And I said, 'Oh, I'm feeding the baby,' and Big Bird said, 'That's a funny way to feed a baby.' And I explained, the baby gets to have everything he needs and I get to cuddle him, and some babies drink from a bottle but this is another way that you can feed a baby, and Big Bird, like a typical little kid said, 'Oh, that's nice' and kept going. So again, they just had the gentlest, most direct touch."[151]

Breastfeeding was usually a taboo topic for television audiences. Buffy remembers being awakened in the hospital after giving birth to Cody. Her nurses showed her a whole stack of promotional literature from baby formula companies. Buffy's doctor assumed she would go along with that choice. Instead, Buffy chose to breastfeed but she needed help. Mothers, grandmothers, and aunties no longer taught their daughters how to breast-feed, so women stopped doing it and babies lost all the benefits that come with the practice. Buffy contacted the La Leche League to learn what to do. The League asked if it could use her picture in its promotional material. Buffy was more than happy to oblige.

Meanwhile, back on *Sesame Street*, Buffy and her family held a little powwow using a local New York drum group, the Silverbird Singers. Buffy enjoyed doing special scenes with Oscar the Grouch and with the Count. Sheldon taught the Count how to count in Dakota, and Buffy taught him how to count in Cree. She also liked to work with Grover, a shy little blue character, and she enjoyed using the show to talk about self-esteem issues.[152]

Buffy left *Sesame Street* in 1980 after the Reagan administration cut back on the cultural funding that had allowed the show to travel. Its subsequent activities would be largely confined to the New York City area, and leaving home was not something Buffy and Cody wanted to do. In fact, when Cody was small, Buffy often took him with her to concerts, where he was sometimes seen asleep in her open guitar case.

In 1989, working from home in Hawaii and in Los Angeles with her friend Jill Frazer, another electronic music pioneer, Buffy created the movie soundtrack for *Spirit of the Wind*, about George Attla, the famous Alaskan dog sled driver. The all-Indian cast included actor and Native American icon, Chief Dan George.

By the end of the 1970s, Buffy and Sheldon Wolfchild had drifted apart. In addition to pursuing separate careers, it was rumoured he had trouble adjusting to the forests of Kauai, which brought back unsettling memories of Vietnam. Wolfchild went on to pursue a successful acting career in Los Angeles. In 1982 he appeared in the movie *Two Against the Wind* and played a Sioux warrior in *Dances with Wolves* (1990). He was Bloody Knife in the 1991 TV production of *Son of the Morning Star*, played Moosshawset in Disney's *Squanto: A Warrior's Tale* (1994), and made an appearance in the 1996 TV movie, *Crazy Horse*. Wolfchild also made guest appearances on *LA Law* and *Star Trek: The Next Generation*.

In 2004, Wolfchild turned once again to politics, launching a successful major lawsuit against the United States over mismanagement of property originally intended for the benefit of the Mdewakanton Sioux of Minnesota.

Buffy continues to be curious about anything that will make colour or sound, and in particular electronic musical instruments. She astounded the arts community with her late-1960s album *Illuminations*, and is adept at using an array of emerging instruments for scoring movies and writing songs. These include the Aarp, the Bouccla, the Moog synthesizer, the Continental Baroque organ, the Mellatron console, and just about anything else Buffy can make go. In the early 1980s, Buffy was comfortable with both the Fairlight and Synclavier music computers and she was in a perfect position to discover the ultimate power tool to maximize her creativity and ability to communicate. Long story short, Buffy fell irreversibly in love with the fledgling Mac computer.

The first Macintosh personal computer went on sale in January 1984. It was the first computer to use graphical user interface and mouse control. Buffy gratefully embraced the new technology, using it to create paintings, music, and writings—eventually she would be one of first artists to have her own Web site. Buffy still owns that original Mac.

During the early 1980s, Buffy used a Fairlight computer adapted to work with music. When the Mac II came out a few years later, with a colour monitor and the PixelPaint program, Buffy expanded into the world of digital art, doing things that had not previously been done. She described it as a delicious experiment, with access to a phenomenal 32 million colours and emerging software like Adobe Photoshop.

"Most people see computers as calculators but pixels can be viewed as blobs of paint." Buffy maintains, however, that the computer does not generate the art; it is just a tool. "The artistic process in digital art is very much the same as for making other kinds of paintings, and I go back and forth in the same painting using both my "wet" studio and my Mac. Artists choose tools; we choose paints; we choose paper or canvas or other media; we have an idea; we start painting; the idea grows as we paint; we work on the painting until at some point we decide the painting is done.

"As an artist, I tended to be fleeing from the noise and the predators that I see all the time in both private and professional life. I do well, but then I need a place to have a real life. Because when I have that time and space and an empty canvas, I fill it with art. It's not work for me—it's the reward. The creativity is natural. If we are made in the image of the Creator, then we are creative.[153]

Buffy feels that the definition of an artist includes simple, natural childhood ingenuity. She muses that if we were to go to the beach with the mindset of a five-year-old, we would use our imaginations to dance, sing, and make drama, stories, sand castles,

Buffy and Cody in Kauai

and pictures in the sand—with no lessons needed at all. Buffy believes that children who are playing and expressing themselves are very close to the artistic spirit that guides everyone.

"I really do love art—it's what I escape to, it's what I flee to. If anything is wrong with me and I am feeling lousy, a bath, a nap, and an empty canvas, it's all I need.[154]

"Asleep and awake, I dream about manipulating colours and shapes and sounds and rhythm. I earn my living giving concerts and speeches; when I'm done, I'm just hungry for pieces of pure sound and pixels of colour, so I take my imagination into my studio and play with sound, and I paint with light.

"An artist who creates lots of work probably experiences prolific days and slower days. Inspiration and energy fluctuations aside, in my own case, I'm now faster on my computer than I am with my traditional water-and-brushes set-up, partly because of enthusiasm. What a computer does is just help me to remember. It helps me to remember so that I can store in my computer, and my computer is remembering things, and this leaves a big hole in my consciousness so that other things can come in."[155]

Buffy's huge, shiny, reflective pieces appeared at the Emily Carr College of Art and Design exhibition in Vancouver in 1994. San Francisco columnist, critic, and computer enthusiast Howard Rheingold who, among other things, founded *The Whole Earth Catalog*, wrote about Buffy's music and her digital art in his Tomorrow column. Buffy told him that a true artist will satisfy the creative urge by making music on pots and pans or by composing for an orchestra, by making images in the sand with a finger, or by manipulating light with a computer.[156] For Buffy, real art occurs in the imagination, using any tools the artist can get his or her hands on.

For the painting *Self-Portrait*, Buffy imported a photo of herself into her computer and experimented. It was a head shot in which she was wearing a lightweight veil with black hair against a blackened background. She painted streaks of bright spectrum computer colours into some feathers. The 1.8 m (6ft.) self-portrait that resulted was included in a series of images in the 1996 exhibition *Painting with Light*, curated by Linda Genereux at First Canadian Place in Toronto.[157]

Buffy rebuts art critics who feel that digital art does not take any effort and is not real art. She notes that digital artists can use a mouse just as other artists use a paintbrush or a pencil. If one has chosen to tell the computer that the stylus is to behave like a piece of chalk, or a pen, or a wet brush, it will. The only real difference is that the drawing shows up on the computer screen. On the computer, one is able to choose the shape of the brush, how wet or gooey the "paint" is, whether the canvas is bumpy or smooth, etc. And there are 32 million colours to choose from, she marvels. Some of those colours are so luminescent that they can't be accurately reproduced by traditional print methods. Painting on a computer monitor screen is literally painting with light.

Some of Buffy's paintings begin with brushes and paints in her "wet" studio. Then she may scan that image into her Mac before manipulating, processing, and further developing the image. She may then print it back out into the real world, add more paint in her wet studio and go back and forth between the two worlds— wet and digital. Digital painters have many options when it comes to making reproductions. Choices may range from the economical to the very expensive. Computer images can be printed on one's own colour printer, or transferred to a professional printing company via disk or File Transfer Protocol (FTP), where they can be produced any way desired.

As with traditional artwork, Buffy sometimes stops and then

comes back to the painting to make changes. She may work on an image for months, even years, just as she does with songs. Generally, she spends about six hours at a time when she's painting but does not tire of putting in more time. The key is in remaining aloof enough from a painting so that you know when to stop, she claims.

"All those colors in your palette are hard for any artist, especially the beginner, to turn down. Once an artist explores the vast variety of tools and features available on the great programs, we're hooked. It's like owning your own art supply store. It's extremely tantalizing to any artist's imagination. You can never misplace or run out of brushes, paints, papers, etc."

Buffy is certainly not oblivious to the practical advantages of digital art. "Another great convenience is certainly the setup-cleanup factor. When I am inspired to paint (or make music) on my Mac, I walk over to the computer, sit down, turn on three switches, and I'm ready to paint or record. It takes me two minutes to go from doing something else to actually painting. If I'm interrupted, it's just a minor inconvenience, but not a disaster, because it's easy to get back where I was: that is, the paint has not changed consistency; the light has not moved. When I'm done, I click save and I'm ready to quit and go back to doing something else. No cleaning up, washing brushes, protecting half-wet paintings from accidents."[158]

Buffy is also attracted to the relationship between photography and painting. In the artist's mind these elements are not always easy to merge. "Visual artists used to fall into one of two categories: those who applied stuff onto other stuff, with brushes or other tools and those who created images with cameras. Digital art software has now empowered both the painterly side of photographers and the photographic side of painters. Digital imaging allows both groups to apply their talents to creating images limited only by their imaginations."

Using Photoshop and other art software, Buffy creates or imports images that she modifies with a kaleidoscope of colours to give depth and wonderment. Some of the creations are as tall as 2.7 m (9 ft).

"The final painting can be both digital and non-digital, going in and out of the wet studio, and in and out of the computer. I end up with a very high-gloss image. After that I may paint on it with metallic dyes. Eventually it hangs on the wall, looking like it's both reflective and very depth-y—like new-car paint."[159]

Examples of Buffy's work include *Pink Village*, a nearly 1.2 by 1.5 m (4x5 ft.) image of a Native Elder looming above a valley with teepees in the background. Its colours are hot pinks and other fragmented hues. The message is one of wisdom bearing witness to chaos and destruction. Another painting, *Wesakechak The Trickster*, represents the supernatural personage described in Native legends as the "sacred fool," who at various times can be funny, obscene, or dangerous. The artwork is a grey-scale image of an unrecognizable human face. *Elder Brothers*, at 2 by 2.5 m (7x8 ft.), is an image of two young Native men who look like wraiths from the 1880s set against an abstract background. *Mohawk Warrior Contemplating the Future* is an image of a Mohawk boy, face and body painted in the traditional way, but re-imaged in teal greens. He is surrounded by other potential selves, cast in rich reds and browns. *Hands: the Coming of the Digital Age* is a self-portrait in greens and blues, red and white. The heavily pixilated image received rave reviews at the *Pixel Pushers* exhibit at the Emily Carr College of Fine Art in Vancouver in 1994.

Buffy's observations on political corruption, greed, and control are not limited to music, or to criticizing colonials. In her painting *Talk Lies*, a fictional Native American man sits like a king, owning everything, giving away nothing. This affected aloofness is the antithesis of a traditional chief. In *Forced to Dance*, an American Indian woman reluctantly dances, back to the viewer, head bowed and hands bound behind her back. A spider is visible untying the cords that bind her wrists. Corrupt-looking men like concrete bureaucrats lounge on tree limbs and self-made pedestals along the edges of the picture. Beams of light emanate from their minds to the dancing woman they think they control.

Buffy's themes also relate to the place she calls home. *Liquid Sunshine* is a fantasy image made for children. In it, dolphins play in a peach-coloured ocean off the island of Kauai. In *Neon Hula*, three dancers are outlined in neon. *Fallen Angels* is a digitized portrait of two Buffys, arms intertwined. The black-and-white image was duplicated and reversed, coloured with cosmic spheres. As in many of Buffy's other digital artworks, the images have a distinctly dream-like quality.

In an early opinion piece called "Cyberskins," that she wrote at the Banff Centre, Buffy comments on how the digital age can be used by Indigenous peoples for their own ends. She believes that the digital scene in Indian country at the moment is a microcosm of the larger picture, with people at various stages of expertise and enthusiasm passing through a great shift. Questions of control and ownership of content and message arise just as they do in mainstream art, but for Native Americans, these are more critical given the facts of Native history. The specter of digital colonialism can frighten many, but Buffy is convinced Native intellectuals, educators, artists, elders, women, tribal leaders, and business people now have many more opportunities to counterbalance past misinterpretations with positive realities, and to replace past exploitations with future opportunities. Buffy wants to see Indian people rise to take advantage of the potential of this new technology, and she is willing to lead by example.[160]

Buffy's digital art has been exhibited in art galleries as diverse as the Institute for American Indian Arts in Santa Fe, New Mexico, Calgary's Glenbow Museum, Toronto's Isaacs Gallery, the Tucson Art Museum in Arizona, the Emily Carr University of Art and Design in Vancouver, and the McKenzie Art Gallery in Regina, Saskatchewan. Her expertise is in demand and she has been happy to share her experiences. Buffy has been Adjunct Professor at the Saskatchewan Indian Federated College (now First Nations University of Canada) in Regina, York University in Toronto, and Evergreen State College in Washington State, as well as at the Institute for American Indian Arts in Santa Fe.

In 1981 Buffy's alma mater, the University of Massachusetts,

Buffy stands in front of her work, *Elder Brothers*, an image of two young Native men who look like wraiths set against an abstract background.

accorded Buffy an honorary doctorate degree in Fine Arts, recognizing her cutting-edge work in digital art and the role of digital technology in the lives of Aboriginal peoples. Her work was acknowledged for the academic merit it demonstrated outside the walls of the university.[161]

Buffy knows from her own experience the value of universities. When talking about her college education, Buffy notes she has managed to continue studying what first interested her in college, and that has enabled her to do things other than "show business" as an artist, a process that keeps her happy.

One of the things that gave Buffy great satisfaction was learning how to apply computers to school education. As she experimented with computers during the 1980s, Buffy found ways to make Native and non-Native kids electronic pen pals using computers, before e-mail existed. She describes how she became involved in the creation of an Indigenous curriculum for children, and how she got the idea of sharing it online:

"When my son Cody was in Grade 5 and we were finished with *Sesame Street*, we were living in Hawaii, and his Grade 5 teacher, Adrya Siebring, came to me and in an embarrassed kind of way said, 'I'm required by law to teach this Indian unit and I know it's baloney,' and God bless her, she did know it was baloney. And she showed me the materials and they were the same junk that I had seen growing up. She asked for my help in presenting a better Indian Studies Unit to her class."[162]

Buffy took a look at Seibring's materials, then went to the

library to confirm how historically biased, outdated, and often downright boring these resources were. The materials were not at all helpful in presenting an accurate or realistic picture of contemporary Indigenous peoples. So Buffy began to write a new unit about Aboriginal peoples and to expand its scope beyond history. She wanted to give fifth-graders a taste of the richness she herself had experienced in Indian country. Buffy wanted to give students an appreciation of Natives' real lives and experiences. In doing so, she began to use the Internet in ways that few teachers were willing to try. She says that what Internet pioneers like John Barlow, Tim Berniers Lee, Bill Gates, Steve Jobs, and Mitch Kapor knew about, few in the public, let alone educators, did.

Buffy put the fifth-grade class in Hawaii in touch, online, with a class at the Starblanket Reserve in the Qu'Appelle Valley, Saskatchewan, where her cousin was teaching.

"And it all came alive. All of a sudden we not only had the curriculum text and the pictures and movies that I had been developing, but we also had children communicating with other children across cultural lines. They would be exchanging faxes, they would be exchanging goodie boxes of local materials, they'd write pen-pal letters, and do self-identity videos they'd exchange. So the text and pictures part wasn't a new idea but when they were all of a sudden communicating live online through what today would be called text messaging, it was very early for that. We had kids on the Internet before most people knew there was an Internet, and for all the right reasons ... We started building cross-cultural friendships online, internationally, from an Aboriginal school in Saskatchewan, putting them in a leadership position of delivering their own self-identity, who they are, to a multicultural, non-Indian class in Hawaii."[163]

The 1980s combining of new Native American core curriculum with cross-cultural distance learning developed into what would eventually become the Cradleboard Teaching Project.

As part of this overall teaching effort, Buffy also finished her first children's book, *Tapwe and the Magic Hat*, in 1986. It is the story of a young Cree boy who leaves his reserve and explores the world with the help of his magic hat. It was undoubtedly inspired by Cody, ten years old at the time and excited about discovering his Native American roots.

On a lighter side, during this period of Buffy's life, Ben Cohen of Ben & Jerry's Ice Cream inducted her, along with singers Carlos Santana and Pete Seeger, Jesuit activist Daniel Berrigan, Bobby Seale (cofounder of the Black Panther Party), Dolores Huerta (of Caesar Chavez's United Farm Workers Union), and several others into B&J's Ice Cream for Life Club. Spike Lee filmed them all in a commercial for new "social activist" flavours, such as Aztec Harvest. For months in 1994, Buffy Sainte-Marie's picture graced national magazines and the buses and subways of New York City. Thanks to the Ice Cream for Life program, Ben & Jerry's ice cream has been served to thousands of Cradleboard Teaching Project Native American youth.

CHAPTER 9

RETURN
TO THE LIMELIGHT

In 1980 Buffy reconnected with arranger, composer, and producer Jack Nitzsche. During the early 1960s, Nitzsche had landed a job as a music copyist at Specialty Records where he met Sonny Bono, then an executive at the record label. Bono encouraged Nitzsche in his early attempts at songwriting. Jack co-wrote "Needles and Pins" with Bono in 1962; the song became a hit for both Jackie DeShannon and The Searchers. As Nitzsche's reputation grew, he began working with Phil Spector, who had moved his recording operations to Los Angeles in 1962. Nitzsche became Spector's first-choice arranger and, by extension, one of the architects behind Spector's Wall of Sound, as he worked on classic releases by the Crystals, the Righteous Brothers, the Ronettes, and Ike and Tina Turner.

After befriending the Rolling Stones in 1964, Nitzsche began leaving his mark on their work, playing keyboard and percussion on early recordings, like "Jumping Jack Flash." Nitzsche played piano in many of the Rolling Stones' 1960s hits, such as "Paint it Black" and "(I Can't Get No) Satisfaction." He was considered somewhat of a backroom genius in the pop scene. Nitzsche's friendship with Neil Young led to Young's recruiting him as a producer and also a touring member of Crazy Horse, for which he wrote string arrangements and played piano. But Nitzsche's stellar reputation as an arranger and composer contrasted with a private life increasingly marred by alcoholism, drug abuse, and a sometimes violent temper. In 1979 he was arrested for pistol-whipping then-girlfriend actress Carrie Snodgress and threatening to kill her. He was fined and sentenced to three years probation for assault with a deadly weapon.

Buffy had first met Nitzsche after Vanguard owner Maynard Solomon put them in touch in the 1960s. The 1970 soundtrack for the film *Performance*, featuring Mick Jagger, listed Nitzsche as music producer and Buffy on vocals for the song "Dyed, Dead, Red" and playing the mouthbow in "Hasishin." Nitzsche had also produced her popular 1971 album *She Used to Wanna be a Ballerina*. Even back then, Nitzsche was admittedly obsessed with Buffy. Whatever it was, when they reconnected in the spring of 1980, she didn't realize that perhaps something about his interest might not be healthy. She hadn't seen Nitzsche for many years until that spring when he happened to be visiting Hawaii. He was working on the score for *An Officer and a Gentleman* but was having trouble coming up with a main theme. Buffy played him a song she had been working on. She recounts how she and Nitzsche and Will Jennings wrote the Academy Award–winning song "Up Where We Belong":

"I had written this little song on my piano, this little melody, and my friend Jack came to visit and told me that he was scoring this movie. Jack's a very famous and incredibly wonderful film composer and he was scoring *An Officer and a Gentleman*. Jack was just worried, very humble, saying. 'I don't have a melody; I'm getting nowhere.' He was a typical film composer thinking he was going to fail; you know, such a hard job, we all think we're going to fail. So I played him what became the hook and the bridge for 'Up Where We Belong.' I had put this strange progression in the middle of it, but it was a very simple kind of melody until you get to that bridge part that says, 'time goes by, no time to cry, life's you and I alive.'"[164]

Nitzsche loved it and played Buffy's song for Taylor Hackford, the film's director. At first Nitzsche was afraid to tell Taylor that it was Buffy who had come up with the original melody. So Buffy kept quiet and didn't say anything every time they saw Taylor. Eventually Nitzsche had to own up.

"People were very surprised to hear I had anything to do with that song. If you really want people to hear about things, you hire a publicist or your record company hires a publicist. These things are just part of the marketplace. Will Jennings is really the one who deserves a huge credit for that song because he took a bit of Jack's verse melody, then he put it together with my hook and bridge and added words. And Stewart Levine did an incredible arrangement, and Joe Cocker and Jennifer Warnes sang it so well. It's such a great record; it became a number one hit all over the world."[165]

It had been a few years since Buffy and Sheldon had drifted apart, each pursuing their careers. Buffy remembers Nitzsche reached her emotionally through Cody, spending time playing with her son and giving him attention. In reality Nitzsche was not a great father figure. But he was a friend from years before, and Buffy appreciated his attention to Cody, although she did not realize how portentous the visit from Nitzsche would be in providing the next step in her personal and professional life.[166]

Buffy, Nitzsche, and Will Jennings accepted the 1982 Academy Award for Best Song from a Motion Picture for "Up Where We Belong," sung by Joe Cocker and Jennifer Warnes, at the ceremony held at the Dorothy Chandler Pavilion in Los Angeles.

Love lift us up where we belong
Where the eagles cry on a mountain high
Love lift us up where we belong
Far from the world we know
Up where the clear winds blow
"Up Where We Belong"

It was a high-profile, albeit brief, comeback to the music industry. The Academy Awards, popularly known as the Oscars, are the most prominent film awards in the world. Granted by the Academy of Motion Picture Arts and Sciences, awards are determined by the Academy's large voting membership. Although it was a great honour for Buffy to win the award, her experience

Buffy with the 1982 Academy Award for Best Song from a Motion Picture for "Up Where We Belong"

was tainted by Nitzsche's behaviour, and it was rumoured that Buffy did not appear at the dinner following the awards ceremony because Nitzsche was high on something and had become argumentative and abusive. Some who saw her after the ceremony thought that Buffy "didn't seem herself." Nevertheless, Buffy and Nitzsche were married later in 1982. Buffy still proudly displays the Oscar statue, which depicts a knight with sword standing on a reel of film.

Buffy relocated to Los Angeles for the early part of this new marriage, putting her career on the back burner. Nitzsche's career overshadowed hers, but he was still possessive and jealous. When he was drinking, Nitzsche insisted that Buffy had no right to call herself a songwriter and that she should know her place. Nitzsche believed he was more successful, wealthier, and more famous. When sober, Nitzsche adored Buffy, but it seemed she could never be perfect enough. His alcohol and drug abuse made Buffy's life difficult: "That part was not good. He was a very hard person to get along with ... lots of problems. We were very different."[167] Only too late did Buffy realize that despite their mutual love of creativity, marrying Nitzsche had not been her best decision.

During the early years of the marriage, Buffy made few appearances or performances. She lent her talents to creating soundtracks and setting up scoring paper for use in Jack's movie productions, basically secretary work. This was a task she did not relish—working under pressure-cooker conditions, without the opportunity to explore her own creativity. Buffy contributed music to the soundtracks for *Starman* (1984), a story about an alien come to Earth, and *The Jewel of the Nile* (1985), a story of a hunt for lost treasure, although she was not given official credit for her work.

Buffy helped Nitzsche financially with the purchase of his house in Studio City in the San Fernando Valley, but wisely kept her farm in Hawaii. When the couple travelled to Hawaii, Buffy hoped that the Kauai environment would have a beneficial effect on Nitzsche's often cantankerous mood and disposition. The cyclical nature of his problems continued, however, and over the next six years, Buffy's life with him in California became intolerable. Fearing for her and her son's safety, Buffy finally fled the house in the middle of one night in the late 1980s and was driven to the airport by a friend. Once in Hawaii, she soon ended the marriage.

After the dissolution of Buffy's relationship with Nitzsche at the end of the 1980s, things went downhill for him. During the mid-1990s, he was caught clearly inebriated on an episode of TV reality crime show *Cops*, brandishing a gun at some youths who had stolen his cap. Nitzsche tried to assuage the police by telling them that he was an Academy Award winner. His hard-living life would eventually take its toll. In 2000 Nitzsche died at age sixty-three of heart failure brought on by a recurring bronchial infection.

Reflecting on her marriage to Nitzsche, Buffy admits that she has always been challenged by her most intimate relationships, and has felt perplexed by this fact, wondering if the problem stems from the abuse she experienced in her childhood. As the difficult domestic relationship with Nitzsche ended, Buffy was free to be active within the Native American community.

"After some time, I realized there is an Indian movement ongoing all the time—people are trying to find solutions to their problems. What we need to do now is put a spotlight on Indian joy and beauty. So, on the reserves I was singing 'Native North American Child,' listing nations and tribes by name—just getting to feel good about ourselves … You see kids laughing and having a good time. Everyone thinks that they have to be serious all of the time to be Indians. But there's always that sense of hope, power, and joy that has inspired me that I have found in sweat lodges, at Friendship Centres, at powwows, and in the homes of friends and relatives."[168]

At this point in her career, Buffy had had plenty of time to rethink things and reconsider her songs' messages: "As proud as I am of my generation for having helped to stop the Vietnam War, there's something we missed doing. Colleges of diplomacy don't exist, but there are colleges of war. Where are our colleges of peace? It's not enough to just write a song, get famous, if we still have war. We have to do more in the rest of our lives—build colleges of peace. Learn how to strategize alternative conflict resolution and diplomacy. I don't think that a song can be the whole solution to a problem. There's too much money in making war. They'll tell you nobody wants a war, but that's not true. Some guys really profit on war and some people will feed their children into that myth before they realize that they're being duped."[169]

Buffy's road toward recording a comeback album had a rather

unusual origin in the Iran-Contra scandal, which played out on television screens from 1983 to 1988, an event which Buffy watched from her living room in Hawaii. The scandal involved the covert American sale of arms to Iran, locked at the time in a desperate war with Iraq. Part of the process included transfers of revenues from the Iran sales to the Contras, a right-wing group fighting the leftist Sandinista government of Nicaragua.

One individual in particular, Major General Richard Secord, caught Buffy's attention. Secord had flown combat missions in Asia in the 1960s. After retiring from the U.S. Air Force, he cofounded a military arms company connected to Lieutenant Colonel Oliver North, the key player in the scandal. In 1987 Secord testified (with no immunity) before the Select Iran–Contra Committee, where he provided a considerable amount of frank and truthful testimony of what had transpired. Buffy was so impressed with Secord's forthrightness that she began to re-evaluate her attitudes toward people in authority. Secord was eventually convicted of involvement in the affair and received two years' probation. Buffy became interested enough to seek out and contact him. In 1992 he became the subject of her song "Fallen Angels."

You believe in the system from the top on down
Potential is a beautiful thing
It's hard to keep believing in the big time
Now you're sinking in the wind
Star light, star bright

Somebody going down tonight

Told the truth when it was time to lie

Got it right

Fallen Angels

Doncha wanna turn em around, turn em around.

"Fallen Angels"

Buffy got to know Richard Secord, his wife JoAnn, and their children. During this time, Buffy was also spending weekends working for Jesse Jackson's campaign for the Democratic nomination to run for president.

Buffy began to think about how her music could inspire people again. She wasn't the type to wait around for government grants or other hand-outs. She believed that the only way to get something done was to tackle the problem herself. She had integrity and the will to follow through on her social convictions. And she was generous with time that could otherwise have been used to make money for personal profit:

"The shows that I was doing on reservations, they were really political as far as content goes. What I was trying to do through my music was to bridge the gap between the reserve and the city, between Native culture and the rest of the world's culture. When I had a bit of money to take myself to places where they couldn't afford me, I'd just be showing up and trying to help people to put on a benefit concert to raise money for something they wanted to do."[170]

Buffy with Major General Richard Secord

In 1984 Buffy had enjoyed narrating *Broken Rainbow,* a documentary about the relocation of 10,000 Navajo and Hopi in Arizona in order to allow the redrawing of reservation boundaries so corporations could access the resource wealth of oil, coal, and uranium. The documentary portrayed the machinations of politicians like John McCain and the accompanying legion of lawyers. The cost of Native American relocation, not including the aftermath of human disruption, came to well over $500 million. *Broken Rainbow* won the 1985 Oscar for Best Documentary.

With the help of Roger Jacobs, whom Buffy credits as her "tech angel," Buffy also continued to shape her music on computer. She had had a home studio in the soundproofed basement of her house on Kauai for years. Contrasting with the "old days" where a studio had to be big and cluttered with equipment, the studio contained minimal equipment: Buffy's Macintosh II computer, MIDI keyboards, and guitars. And with this she was able to carry on as she always had—to think differently, as the Macintosh slogan went. Buffy had learned how to create and deliver music in digital form years before with the Synclavier and the Fairlight, early music computers she'd used for film scoring. The Macintosh made her digital art and music portable. To someone who travelled as Buffy did, using her computer for professional-level home recordings that she could place on disks and carry in her purse, the Mac became a very special instrument.

In 1990, Buffy's attorney and friend Abe Somer had heard Buffy's homemade demos and played them for friends Nigel Grainge and Chris Hill, who owned Ensign Records, a subdivision of Chrysalis Records in England. Grainge and Hill became interested in Buffy's demos. Grainge suggested she might want to work with Chris Birkett, who was based in London and was working with Sinead O'Connor on what would be her hit, "Nothing Compares to You." However, Buffy found herself faced with the challenge of living in Hawaii, virtually on the opposite side of the world from her proposed music producer. She challenged Ensign Records to do something they had never done before, to help Buffy and Birkett work together from opposite ends of the globe. Buffy found a way to send her songs from her home studio using satellite technology. She and Roger Jacobs, her engineer, recorded her songs into the computer, then sent them on telephone line via modem to be bounced off a satellite and land on tape in London. Musical Instrument Digital Interface (MIDI) does not transmit sound, but rather a digital description of the sound, which can be changed back into musical form.

Birkett elaborates on the process: "Before the Internet was invented [popularized] ... there was a system called Compuserve, which was a satellite data transmission situation. However, it wasn't very high resolution. So we used to send MIDI files back and forth to each other. I had a studio in London and Buffy had her studio in Hawaii and she sent me these MIDI files of new songs, with written explanations and notes ... I put them into my system, and her demos came up exactly how she was doing them in Hawaii, directly in my London studio. So I recorded some of it onto a twenty-four-track tape."[171]

This exchange between Birkett and Buffy is believed to be the first documented use of the Internet for sending music files across the Internet, from one of the most isolated places in the middle of the Pacific Ocean all the way to the other side of the globe. Buffy and Roger Jacobs later travelled to Birkett's studio in England, where Buffy recorded most of her final vocals and mixes.

Buffy's fifteenth album, *Coincidence and Likely Stories*, was released by Chrysalis/Ensign in 1991. This album continued to incorporate a pop sound and was politically provocative. Buffy's sound and lyrics reflected further emotional evolution and a deeper exploration of greed and politics, as in the songs "The

Big Ones Get Away," "Fallen Angels," "Disinformation," and the scathing "Priests of the Golden Bull." The song "The Big Ones Get Away," focused on political intrigue and was a hit in the United Kingdom. The title was a veiled reference to the role played by Presidents Ronald Reagan and George H.W. Bush, and Lieutenant Colonel Oliver North in the Iran-Contra Affair. The major players got away with it (North was granted immunity), while the honest ones, such as Secord, did not. Regarding her new song "Fallen Angels," Buffy had once thought that people at the top of the heap were inhuman. She hadn't understood them and admits that, pre-Secord, she had been a little naïve and judgmental. After spending time with General Secord, who did exactly as he was told by whichever president was in office, she came to a new understanding of the relationship between the military and political power.

It was not until nearly twenty years after Anna Mae Aquash's death that Buffy was finally able to express her feelings and sense of outrage in the song "Bury My Heart at Wounded Knee." Anna Mae had been the highest-ranking woman in the American Indian Movement and was murdered, execution-style, on the Pine Ridge Indian Reservation in South Dakota in 1975. It was widely believed that the federal government was covering up evidence relating to the killer. Buffy wanted answers. (In 2010, former AIM member John Graham was convicted of the murder of Aquash.)

Buffy understands that few performers have been able to assume the mantle of activism with the tough lyrics and mass

The cover art for *Coincidence and Likely Stories*

exposure as she has done. To write songs like "Universal Soldier" or "Bury My Heart at Wounded Knee," one must have the passion and experience the incidents that nobody wants to hear about, she believes.[172]

Buffy challenges authority on behalf of those who have been victimized. But that can be a dangerous thing to do. As Robbie

Robertson says: "Some people in power become dangerous, there's too much money, too much power involved. Buffy came up with another great way of describing it: They're power junkies like in 'The Big Ones Get Away.' They hire all the smart ones, and that is the way it works. You don't step too much on the toes of power junkies or you pay. Some pay with lives. Anna Mae Aquash paid with her life, and Leonard Peltier is paying two lifetimes for a crime he claims he did not commit. And Buffy gets in there and she has a way of bringing this forward."[173]

Coincidence and Likely Stories also includes the song "Starwalker," which salutes Native American spirit and spirituality. Buffy first wrote "Starwalker" in 1975, around the time that her albums were being banned, and the song only became a major hit when rereleased in Europe in 1991. It represents a new genre that incorporates a traditional Native American sound into a pop context, for which Buffy had coined the term "powwow rock." Record companies were reluctant to embrace the concept, but Buffy insisted this type of song be included in her albums. Buffy says that Starwalker is not a specific person, but he is the hero that everyone sees. Buffy attracted 90,000 people to a concert in Paris in 1993 that featured her synthesized music. She was named France's Best International Artist for that year. Buffy was presented the prestigious Grand Prix Charles De Gaulle in recognition of the *Coincidence* album.

Starwalker he's a friend of mine

You've seen him looking fine

He's a straight talker

He's a Starwalker, don't drink no wine

Wolf Rider she's a friend of yours

You've seen her opening doors

She's a history-turner, she's a Sweetgrass burner

And a Dog Soldier

Ay hey way hey wey heya

Holy Light, guard the night

Pray up your medicine song

Oh, straight dealer you're a spirit healer

Keep going on

Ay hey way hey wey heya

Lightning Woman, Thunderchild

Star soldiers one and all oh

Sisters, brothers all together

Aim straight, stand tall

"Starwalker" (2003)

Chris Birkett describes Buffy as being a very strong artist who knows what she is doing, one who uses her intuition via emotions to create an environment that is not pre-planned: "I was very much into cultural music, cultural communications and education of the masses through the medium of music of cultural peoples. That's the type of thing that Buffy does. She helps cultures to communicate with each other. I think music is really useful to do that because it's beyond intellect. Music speaks directly to the emotion and the intuition, and that's very important."[174]

On the road, Neil Chapman, who played bass and guitar for Buffy for more than ten years, appreciates not only her depth of knowledge but also her approachability. He says that when you travel around in a van for nine hours with someone, you really get to know them. He describes Buffy as witty and loving to give and take a joke.[175]

Elaine Bomberry, president of the National Aboriginal Recording Industry Association and a major promoter of Aboriginal music talent, remembers the influence Buffy had on her when she was a child: "I had to be around ten or eleven when my parents took us to see her at the taping of her CBC special in Toronto. The Native community had been invited and given free tickets. We went down and I'll never forget it, seeing her in her big platforms. I still remember that she had yellow feathers. They were really bright yellow in her hair. It was just amazing to see and hear her sing her hits, you know, because my parents had her music at home. We had all of her albums at home. To see live television and to see her perform, it really had an impact for me."[176]

Describing the Aboriginal music scene at the time, Bomberry observes that Buffy was about the only Aboriginal person prominent on mainstream television. She didn't recall seeing a lot of other Aboriginal performers other than a Native band called Redbone. Fortunately today there is the Aboriginal People's Television

Network, which provides far more exposure to Native talent.

Bomberry remembers how Buffy played an instrumental role in the development of the Aboriginal Music category of the Canadian Academy of Recording Arts and Sciences Juno Awards in 1992. Out of the blue, Buffy called Bomberry at home to say she had heard through the grapevine that there was a proposal to introduce an Aboriginal category to the Junos. Buffy was wondering if Bomberry could use some help. Bomberry was thrilled and couldn't believe it was Buffy herself making the offer. She immediately accepted. "Shingoose and I met her at her hotel … she had her laptop there and I was just, like, strategy or not, Buffy, you're the first person to walk in that boardroom tomorrow morning. We all agreed on that. Buffy prepared an eloquent speech talking about the significance and the importance of Native music in contemporary Canadian society. She compared it to what was happening with Black music back in the thirties and forties, when they were starting to record in the studios, and making that whole comparison. This is where our music was at. It was so eloquent and beautiful and powerful.

Five representatives, including Buffy, had twenty minutes in total to make their presentation to the academy. They made a philosophical statement on the importance of such a category; they described the number of Aboriginals performing and recording over the years and demonstrated that there was a real burst of activity. After the twenty-minute presentation, the delegation was "kicked out" of the boardroom and stood in the hallway to await the verdict. Elaine says, "Twenty minutes later they brought us back in and said, 'You got the category, but you can't tell anyone for three weeks.' That was the longest three weeks of my life! We couldn't tell a soul."[177]

Despite such positive developments in Canada, there were also large steps being taken backward. Buffy watched with concern as the 1990 Oka Crisis became the most well-publicized violent conflict between First Nations and the Canadian government in the 20th century.

Since the mid-1980s, the Mohawk community of Kanesatake had attempted to negotiate with the town of Oka, Québec, over the expansion of a golf course and residential development that would impinge on traditional and sacred burial grounds. As a protest against a court decision allowing the golf course construction to proceed, the Mohawks blocked Highway 334. About a thousand members of the Sûreté du Québec (SQ), Quebec's provincial police force, were brought in and a decision was made to storm and dismantle the barricades. SQ Corporal Marcel Lemay died during the ensuing exchange of tear gas and gunfire.

The situation continued to escalate as the Kanesatake Mohawks were joined by Natives from across Canada and the U.S. In solidarity, another group of Mohawks at the nearby location of Kahnawake blockaded the Mercier Bridge at the point where it passed through their territory, thus sealing off a major access point between the Island of Montreal and Montreal's heavily populated South Shore suburbs. The SQ established its own blockade on a nearby highway to restrict access to Oka and Kanesatake. Racial epithets flew among the local citizens inconvenienced by the blockades and a Mohawk warrior was burned in effigy among chants of *"sauvages"* (savages). The Mohawk warriors were vilified in the press as terrorists.

The crisis reached a boiling point when, on August 14, the Royal Canadian Mounted Police (RCMP) took over for the SQ. Ten RCMP constables were injured. Then the federal government stepped in. On August 24, a company of the Quebec-based Royal 22e Régiment took over three barricades and arrived at the final blockade leading to the disputed area. Tensions rose as 2,500 army troops tightened the perimeter around the protesters (from 1.5 km to 5 m), slowly constricting their free space.

On August 29, at the Mercier Bridge blockade, the Mohawks negotiated an end to their protest. The golf course expansion was cancelled by the mayor of Oka. The Oka Crisis lasted seventy-eight days.

In some ways, the situation seemed reminiscent of the Wounded Knee occupation. After voluntarily abandoning their positions, the warriors were arrested on charges of weapons possession and assault. In July 1992, a jury acquitted all but three of the participants. Not including the costs incurred by the RCMP, the standoff cost the government $155 million. The aftermath led to a major Royal Commission on Aboriginal Peoples report that took a comprehensive look at issues facing Aboriginal peoples in Canada. Many would later accuse the government of shelving the report's recommendations.

Buffy could only watch helplessly as this drama unfolded. She had a crisis of her own with which to contend.

On September 11, 1992, Hurricane Iniki—the most devastating hurricane to ever hit Hawaii—made a direct hit on Kauai. It was a Category 5 with sustained winds of 200 km (124 mi.) per hour and caused an astounding $2.3 billion in property damage. Waves of up to eleven m (35 ft.) crashed on the island's south shore for hours. Flying sheets of roofing metal were especially dangerous.

Electricity was knocked out for weeks, and telephone and other communications were entirely blacked out, so updated news was hard to come by. Altogether, 1,400 homes were destroyed and more than 5,000 were badly damaged. Steven Spielberg was arranging the final day of shooting for *Jurassic Park* on the island, but was forced to delay because of the storm. Fortunately, warnings had been issued and thousands were able to seek shelter. The number of fatalities was limited to six. Buffy's house was among those that suffered major damage and required extensive repairs. Among the valuable items blown away was the Silver Jubilee Medal from her Command Performance for Queen Elizabeth II in 1977. On a positive note, everyone on the island pitched in and helped others to cope, demonstrating their ability to act as a community.

In Toronto, too, the notion of community reverberated through 1992. Jack Lenz, a composer, keyboardist, and producer, organized the Live Unity concert in Toronto to celebrate diversity of musical expression. Buffy and Dan Seals of Seals and Croft were among the featured performers. Lenz was an adherent of the Bahá'í faith, with its idea of a Universal Creator and its concept of the essential unity of all religions. These ideas were familiar to Buffy, given her university study of world religions. Although Buffy herself is not a Bahá'í, she has appeared at concerts, conferences, and conventions of the Bahá'í religion, such as the musical prelude to the 1992 Bahá'í World Congress, a double concert called "Live Unity: The Sound of the World," captured in a video broadcast and documentary. Also in 1992, Buffy participated in the "De-celebration of Columbus" on the 500th anniversary of Columbus's landing in the Americas. There were representatives of nearly one hundred Indigenous Nations present.

The following year, 1993, was another busy one for Buffy as she assumed a larger role on the international stage, by accepting an invitation from the Canadian Commission for the United Nations Educational, Scientific and Cultural Organization (UNESCO) to act as Spokesperson for the Associated Schools Project Network (ASPnet). The network's mission was to mobilize public and private learning institutions, and develop and participate in pilot projects designed to kindle and foster a culture of peace and tolerance. ASPnet aims to enhance international understanding in order to prepare children and youth to approach the urgent challenges facing humanity.

Buffy also provided an Indigenous presence at the 1993 Roskilde Music Festival in Denmark, which was attended by youth from across Europe (Roskilde is run as a non-profit organization and raises funds for music, culture, and humanist activities. It attracts about 200,000 youth, mainly from Scandinavia). Buffy was a headline performer and brought along a supporting cast of one hundred Native performers from North America. Albert Angus helped to arrange for teepees to be shipped to Denmark to create a unique Native American camp in Europe. That year Buffy also headlined an Indigenous concert in the Sami homelands in Lapland. Danish filmmaker and good friend Stig Thornsohn helped Buffy bring Native American performers over to the Roskilde concert, and the group also visited Norway and Iceland. They erected what was probably the first teepee ever put up in Iceland.

In 1993, Buffy hosted her own CBC television show, *The Many Moods of Buffy Sainte-Marie*, and found time to accept the BRIT Award presented by the British Academy of Film and Television Arts, and the Dove Award offered by the Gospel Music Association. Later, Buffy performed with the National Arts Centre symphony orchestra at the Museum of Civilization in Hull, Québec, receiving "a roaring and deserved" standing ovation.

On a personal level, Buffy found a new relationship in Hawaii. Chuck Wilson recalls how he first met Buffy, when he rebuilt her alarm system after Hurricane Iniki. After he finished the job and went home, there was still a problem with the battery sensor, which kept on beeping. Despite the weekend, Wilson went back to look at the alarm again. Wilson was a single parent with two little kids that he did not want to leave alone, so he called ahead to make sure it was okay to bring his kids along. Buffy must have been impressed by his fatherly impulses. They started talking and, before long, they started going out together.

Wilson admits that, when he first met Buffy, he didn't realize who she was. He liked how she looked and that she was really cheerful to be around. On the positive side, Buffy quickly became "Mommy" to Chuck's two young children, Christopher and Cherelle. Buffy describes what she liked in Wilson: "He had a sense of understanding that I had not seen before. Because I was a tan girl in a white community, and he was a white boy raised in a tan community. He was raised in a solid Hawaiian community. And it was kind of a reverse, but he did have a sense of what it was like to be different and to have to earn respect and to have respect. He was a single parent and had been having a pretty hard time. And, I just said yes to the whole deal."[178]

When Wilson met Buffy, there was little viable fencing left on her property because of the hurricane and Buffy wanted to keep goats. She had liked them since childhood and everywhere she went she was taking pictures of goats. Buffy would even carve goat figures out of guava branches. Wilson ended up putting in almost a mile of new fencing around Buffy's pastures. He thought that having goats at her place would be a good way for Buffy, who tended to get caught up in her projects, to slow down a bit and take time to enjoy some animal companionship.

As Buffy and Wilson got to know each other, her genuine and deep-seated love for animals soon became apparent to him. She says that when she's with an animal, something special happens that is something like bio-feedback. She can turn off her whole internal verbal thing, and then she seems to attain something akin to an alpha-brainwave meditative state. She says that the same thing happens when parents look into their babies' eyes, or when the eyes of lovers lock in a gaze. She finds what occurs when her verbal sense is totally quiet is a little miracle and a great source of healing when she feels stressed. When Buffy is in an airplane and wanting to zone out, she can recall that pet-the-cat feeling again and bring up the same nonverbal heaven. She has learned how to tap into the power of the nonverbal part of her nature.[179] Buffy and Wilson stayed together on her farm for thirteen years, and she helped him raise his children from the primary grades through high school graduation.

Meanwhile, back in Canada, a disturbing shooting in 2005 caught Buffy's attention. The Ipperwash dispute in Ontario stemmed back to 1942, when the Canadian government expropriated land belonging to the Stony Point Indian band under the War Measures Act to build a military camp called Ipperwash. In the ensuing decades, the Stony Point people tried several times to have the land returned, noting that it contained their traditional burial grounds. In 1993 Stony Point band members began to move back onto the abandoned site. By September 1995, when no progress had yet being made, a group of thirty protesters erected a barricade at nearby Ipperwash Provincial Park to emphasize their case.

Ontario Provincial Police (OPP) moved in on the protesters to evict them from the park. There is no agreement on what happened next. The OPP said they had no choice but to draw guns because the protesters were armed. The protesters maintain the opposite, that they were unarmed and that police, in full riot gear, used unnecessary force. Protesters also pointed the finger squarely at Premier Mike Harris, claiming that he pressured the police to rush the barricades in a night-time raid. Whatever the truth, Dudley George, one of the group's leaders, did not survive the assault and died on the scene after being shot by OPP Sergeant Kenneth Deane.

As the information about Dudley George emerged, Buffy was shocked and wanted to know more. The events of George's death and the problems surrounding the lack of a full judicial inquiry preyed on her mind, and Buffy believed it was time for teachers to be able to tell their students exactly what happened at Ipperwash. Buffy headlined a benefit concert at Massey Hall in Toronto to help raise funds for the Ipperwash Justice Fund. Teachers contributed most of the $60,000 raised to help the George family. Eventually Sergeant Deane would be convicted of criminal negligence causing death after a court ruled he could not have had a "reasonable belief" that Dudley George was armed. The federal government has since returned the land to the people.

Back in showbiz, Buffy, a fan of the Iroquois Confederacy, was offered the role of Gesina in the 1994 U.S. television film *The Broken Chain*, starring Pierce Brosnan. The movie recounted the collapse of the Iroquois League of Five Nations during the American Revolutionary War. Floyd Westerman and Wes Studi also played roles. Although all of the Indian players had felt the movie sounded promising on paper, most were unhappy with the final result.

During the same time, Buffy worked with music producer Ted Whitecalf of Sweetgrass Records and traditional Aboriginal round dance group Red Bull of Saskatchewan to promote self-esteem and healthy lifestyles. Whenever there was an opportunity, Buffy would try to get Red Bull and other traditional powwow groups hired on television shows and concerts in which she was involved.

In 1995 Buffy was selected for induction into the Canadian Music Hall of Fame. The Canadian Academy of Recording Arts and Sciences, suggested that Joe Cocker and Jennifer Warnes be invited to sing their award-winning rendition of Buffy's song "Up Where We Belong" to honour her at that year's Juno awards. Buffy countered that she would rather have Stoney Park, a First Nations drum group that sang backup to many of her songs, perform instead.

Elaine Bomberry wanted to add something even more special to honour Buffy: a hundred and two powwow dancers in full regalia. "In early April, around here a lot of families were heading to the first event of our powwow season at Ann Arbor, Michigan. I had to try and convince all of these dancers to come and dance. But once they heard it was for Buffy, that was it. One hundred and two of them changed their plans and came because they loved her. Buffy had no idea these dancers were going to come out during the tribute. There were two aisles coming up to the main stage, and Buffy was so surprised and pleased. We thought the roof was going to come off of the place!"[180]

Buffy stood and watched the surprise spectacle, smiling but overwhelmed and speechless. She was seen wiping tears from her eyes. It was a rare moment of real recognition of the work to which she had devoted so much of her life.

Master of Ceremonies Tom Jackson praised Buffy as a creator, a leader, a scholar, a world visionary, a seeker of justice, and a true guiding spirit. Lee Silversides, president of the Canadian Academy of Recording Arts, lauded Buffy's longevity, the astounding variety of her accomplishments and her causes, all of which he believed merited her induction into the Juno Hall of Fame. Buffy thanked everyone in several Aboriginal languages. She credited much of her inspiration to the people in various small communities across the country such as Waswanipi, Telegraph Creek, Red Deer, and Lumsden, who took in her performances. She urged other performers to escape beyond the spotlights and discover the rest of Canada. Among the individuals Buffy singled out to thank over her career were Sam "The Record Man" Sniderman, who went out of his way to promote Canadian talent and was kind to Buffy in her early career; Dean Cameron, who pulled together her team; and finally, Jack Lenz, whose combination of faith and talent she found inspiring.

Buffy never liked the "star system" and its commercialization as it only further distanced performers from their audience and ordinary people. Buffy touched a lot of people and kept in touch with them; she kept a cassette tape of Charlie Hill from the time he was an aspiring comedian thirty years earlier. When she played it for Hill again, he thought he was awful but was nevertheless amazed that Buffy had kept the tape. Buffy's protest songs empowered other Native musicians, such as Floyd Westerman, who realized that they could also speak out about their own sorrows and triumphs.

Lenz composed the music for the 1995 film *Pocahontas: The Legend*, in which Buffy provided vocals and well-known Cree actor Gordon Tootoosis, and Mohawk Billy Two Rivers had roles. Lenz also executive produced Buffy's sixteenth album, *Up Where You Belong*, released by EMI in 1996. Coproduced by Buffy and Chris Birkett, it features the song for which she won her 1982 Oscar, as well as remakes of earlier hits, "Universal Soldier" and "Until It's Time for You to Go." The album opens with the single "Darling Don't Cry," which Buffy described as a powwow love song, recorded with the Red Bull powwow group from the Little Pine First Nation in Saskatchewan.

In 1997 Buffy received a Gemini Award (Canada's version of an Emmy) for her performance in the CTV television special *Buffy Sainte-Marie: Up Where We Belong*, beating out both Celine Dion and Alanis Morissette. That year she also received the Lifetime Musical Achievement Award from First Americans in the Arts and travelled to Minneapolis to accept long overdue recognition: Philanthropist of the Year, presented as part of the Louis T. Delgado Award for Native American Philanthropy.

In May 1997, Governor-General Romeo Leblanc invested Buffy as an Officer of the Order of Canada, the highest civilian honour in Canada. Also that year she was recognized with the Lifetime Achievement Award from the American Indian College Fund and

Buffy served on Hillary Clinton's Committee to Save America's Treasures.

served on Hillary Rodham Clinton's Committee to Save America's Treasures. In 1999 Buffy also received the National Aboriginal Achievement Award organization's Lifetime Achievement Award.

CHAPTER 10

INSPIRING
A NEW GENERATION

✳

"The Cradleboard Teaching Project was born out of my own experiences as a teacher who has travelled widely, thanks to a concert career. When I had a concert in New York, afterwards I would go to the Mohawk Reservation out in the country upstate. If I had a concert in Sydney, Australia, afterwards I would spend some time with Aboriginal people there. This became a way of life for me, and I'm grateful for all the good people who taught and learned with me across cultural borders."[181]

Buffy had received her teaching certificate in 1962 and would combine her passion for teaching with professional travelling. She started the philanthropic non-profit fund, Nihewan Foundation for American Indian Education, in 1968 with her "left-over singing money," initially to provide scholarships for Native American students. In the 1970s and 1980s she expanded the foundation to serve elementary, middle, and high school students by creating interactive multimedia core curricula through Native American cultural perspectives. Similar to the way she writes songs, Buffy was creating original curriculum materials.

In the mid-1980s, with five years of *Sesame Street* completed, and now divorced from Jack Nitzsche, Buffy and Cody were again living in Hawaii. Cody's Grade five teacher, Adrya Siebring, was required to teach a Native American study unit to Cody's class but she felt she lacked accurate teaching materials and asked for Buffy's help. Buffy looked at what was available and found the archaic curriculum materials to be inadequate, inaccurate, and boring, not at all in keeping with the exciting realities she was experiencing in Indian country. She took on the challenge, put on her teacher's hat again, and wrote up the beginnings of what would become a whole new paradigm in educational curricula. Moreover, she used the new curriculum materials as the basis to partner Siebring's class at Island School in Hawaii with the Starblanket Reserve School at File Hills, Saskatchewan. "Mainstream teachers complain about the lack of enriching accurate teaching materials about Native American people," says Buffy, "and Native American people suffer from being misperceived all their lives by the same lack."[182]

Buffy spent the next twelve years on what would become the pilot for the Cradleboard Teaching Project. She faced many challenges as she expanded the program, and credits Harold Tarbell (Mohawk) of the Akwesasne Reserve with helping her develop the grant proposal for the first phase the project. She made an in-kind contribution of her recording studio in Hawaii, transforming it into the Cradleboard production studio.

"As a teacher who was also a songwriter, I had brought Indian issues to the attention of my own generation through my records. Then in the late '70s I became a semi-regular on *Sesame Street* for five years. I wanted little kids and their caregivers to know one thing above all: that American Indians exist. We are not all dead and stuffed in the museums with the dinosaurs."[183]

To fund Cradleboard's online launch, the Nihewan Foundation received a major grant from the W.K. Kellogg Foundation that was followed by other grants from the Ford Foundation, the Lyn and Norman Lear Family Foundation, the Herb Alpert Foundation, the Toyota USA Foundation, and the Shakopee Mdewakanton Business Council. In-kind contributions have been highly significant, particularly from Rotary Club chapters. These monies were all from American-based foundations and many had mandates that restricted their giving to serving needs within U.S. borders first, but Buffy found ways to include countless items of Canadian content. The American Indian Higher Education Consortium, representing thirty-three tribal colleges, assisted in providing supporting materials.

In 1996, the Cradleboard Teaching Initiative initially launched its pilot project in eleven states and provinces, reaching Mohawk, Cree, Ojibway, Menominee, Coeur d'Alene, Navajo, Quinnault, Hawaiian, and Apache communities, each of whom partnered with a non-Indian class of the same grade level through what now would be called Live Chat.[184] Participating pilot schools came from such diverse locations as the Akwesasne Freedom School in New York State, Alchesay School among the White Mountain Apache of Arizona, Navajo Preparatory School in New Mexico, Rocky Boy

School in Montana, Tahola Public School among the Quinault of Washington State, and White Calf Collegiate in Saskatchewan, with mainstream schools including Johnston Park School in Princeton, New Jersey, Chestnut Hill Academy in Philadelphia, and Sidwell Friends School in Arlington, Virginia. Jon Ord's Kids from Kanata project in Ontario was especially helpful.

Buffy's educational plan envisioned the creation of something new—the Electronic Powwow, an interactive, multimedia, core curriculum of real school subjects taught from within the cultural perspectives of Indigenous people. The additional stroke of genius besides the curriculum was to have it delivered interactively by the Native American pupils themselves to their non-Indian colleagues far away. This put Indian educators and communities into the driver's seat for the first time, delivering their own self-identity and culture as they saw fit, keeping quality control accurate and local.

"Even in good schools, units focusing on Native Americans most often have taken a hobbyist approach, wherein students discover corn, moccasins, the concept of pre-Columbian existence, and the fact that we Indians are 'a thing of the past' like the dinosaurs. But when it came to important subjects like science, social studies and geography, the curriculum goes back to being only Eurocentric. What kind of message does that give to any student about Native American culture? Even more disturbing: what kind of a message does it give to the Native American child about himself or herself?"[185]

The Cradleboard Teaching Project's work builds cross-cultural friendships in schools through study from within Indigenous cultural perspectives, without abandoning the concept of core curriculum (referring to the subjects most educators agree should be taught: science, social studies, history, language and geography). These subjects have no particular ethnicity and therefore culture shouldn't be an obstacle to learning it but rather should help make it more engaging.[186]

"For example with science, every group who has survived has done so because they observed, experimented, remembered, passed on information to younger generations about how things work, where things are, what tools, techniques, inventions, medicines, foods, skills and behaviors are most successful. Cradleboard's science curriculum studies the concepts of frequency and amplitude as part of a unit on the Principles of Sound. Then we reinforce learning by studying Native American musical instruments: why heat changes the sound of the drum, why covering and uncovering holes in the flute changes the pitch. It's an opportunity to study real science concepts from within a Native American cultural perspective."[187]

Even by the mid-1990s, Buffy's determination that the computer could be an excellent vehicle for learning was pretty radical. Most people at the time believed that computers were mostly for accountants and had no vision of computers in the hands of young children, busy classroom teachers, and Indians on reservations. As Buffy's skills in digital music and art kept pace with emerging technologies, her excitement at bringing Native

Buffy spent 12 years working on the pilot for the Cradleboard Teaching Project, which builds cross-cultural friendships in schools through study from within Indigenous cultural perspectives, without abandoning the concept of core curriculum.

American curricula into a colourful multimedia reality grew.

In the late 1980s, Buffy was invited to give a speech at the Women in Philanthropy conference in Montana. It was attended by educator Dr. Valorie Johnson, (Seneca), a program officer at the W. K. Kellogg Foundation. Johnson contacted a mutual friend, Dr. Norbert Hill, an Oneida-Cree educator who had written a study on Buffy's music that postulated that if she had not been so outspoken on Indian issues, Buffy would have had a spectacular career in the United States. Buffy exchanged ideas with Hill and Johnson that would lead to Buffy's working with Harold Tarbell, a former Mohawk chief at

Akwesasne Reserve, to write a proposal to the Kellogg Foundation. Dr. Johnson, who had successfully shepherded American Indian Tribal Colleges partnerships with the W.K. Kellogg Foundation, had a rare understanding of education in Native American communities and saw the Cradleboard Teaching Project as visionary.

Combined with Buffy's Nihewan Foundation resources, the Kellogg Foundation's support allowed the Cradleboard team to hire Native American curriculum developers Orbis Associates, which included Richard Nichols, Gwen Shunatona, and Anne Litchfield. Part of their job was to list grade level facts and concepts, and to schedule Cradleboard's delivery of teaching materials for when students should be studying those things. As a teacher, Buffy knew how busy teachers were and how important it was to "fit" into existing realities in schools already overwhelmed with "extras." The Orbis team found the concept of core curriculum from within a Native American perspective a fascinating new approach. Their text contributions, combined with Buffy's vision and multimedia artistry, resulted in the first round of Cradleboard curricula in government, social studies, and science.

Having delivered her first electronic album in the 1960s and used computers for making music and art, Buffy became a pioneer in the field of what would eventually be called e-learning. Buffy may have been precocious in her use of computers for music, art, and education, but Cradleboard was never just about the technology. The key was always about the content—helping children grow through cross-cultural communication while having a unique opportunity to access engaging, accurate, enriching, core curriculum units that met appropriate standards for elementary, middle, and high school grade levels.

"Kids today sometimes don't want to come to school—it's boring. Teachers are over-tasked, they have these lists that they have to match, they have to go out and do their own research. With the new technologies we could be pooling our resources and giving teachers more time to spend teaching kids by providing accurate content up front.

"At Cradleboard, we use multimedia so there's more of an oral tradition, more multi-sensory learning, and it's much more engaging than text alone. What we're competing with in education is television, drugs, alcohol, movies, sports, and video games, and we should be using some of the new technology to engage students. Local communities can create their own local curriculum about themselves."[188]

Working with teachers and teacher education programs across North America, Buffy was a leader in the new online teaching medium. She believed that teachers could boil a lesson down to brief engaging episodes and present it in an enjoyable way using interactive multimedia and distance connections. A piece of curriculum can have the same power as a well-written, three-minute song when it is brief, focused, and engaging. The new Cradleboard curriculum is multisensory and presented through multimedia— appealing to eyes and ears and the whole brain—and it's fun for the student to use, including those with short attention spans.[189]

Buffy feels that good teachers, like good entertainers, come in many styles. The good ones have in common an ability to understand and deliver the meanings beyond the words. Good teachers seldom need to talk loud, blow whistles, or clap hands for attention, because children are naturally riveted to an engaging educator who has something to say about an interesting subject. The same elements that make showbiz work can be effective in teaching: a sense of truth, humour, colour, motion, sound, a delight in engaging with an audience, charisma, and confidence in the accuracy of what you're saying.

Buffy admits that some teachers are apologetic when they first get involved with Cradleboard because they feel ignorant about Indigenous people's histories and cultures. Others feel guilty or bitter about dealing with the facts of genocide in the Americas. Buffy encourages them with a presentation about Guilt and Bitterness:

Making Things Better by helping children and teachers to deal with Guilt and Bitterness

Guilt and Bitterness are two sides of the same coin. When Native American people begin to learn the painful truth of how unjustly we have been treated, many of us go through a hell of Bitterness. When European Americans learn about it, many people go through a hell of Guilt. Some people will tell you to "Just throw that away, that guilt, that bitterness," but you shouldn't: you should learn to use it. Re-purpose it.

Think of those ancient people out on the Plains. They're carrying bags. They're bending over, picking things up off the prairie. What are they gathering? Food? No. Wood? No. They're collecting dried buffalo chips. That's manure. But it's dried, and that's the key. They take that dried manure that others throw away, and they bring it back home, and then they do the magic that only Human Beings can do: they turn it into fuel; and they make fire.

Once you make fire, you can create light and warmth. It's like you extend the length of the day. You can build a community around a fire; you can read a book beside a fire; you can dream and invent and write a book beside a fire. Or you can cook up something brand new, and all because you were smart enough to convert that dried up manure into fuel to make a fire. Or you can take that dried manure—that Guilt, that Bitterness— and spread it on your garden as fertilizer and grow something brand new. But you have to be patient enough to let Nature dry it out in order to convert it into something positive.

Buffy Sainte-Marie, Cradleboard Teaching Project

The concept of American Indian contributions to world knowledge is absent in most schools. The Cradleboard elementary science unit presents farming techniques and the nutritional value of various foods in a lesson pointing out that nearly two-thirds of the world's important foodstuffs were hybridized, cultivated, and distributed by Indigenous people of the Americas.

"Almost all of the vegetables and fruits that the world's people eat today were *developed* by human beings in the western hemisphere—they weren't just growing wild in the wilderness. Corn is especially interesting. Most texts say things like, "Corn appeared . . ." and most people probably figure that Native Americans found corn already growing there and were smart enough to eat it. The text should say, "Native American people cultivated, hybridized and distributed corn throughout the Americas." Corn is only distributed by human beings, and people have to teach each other how to cultivate it. This is called cultural diffusion ... This concept implies a lot about the sophistication, technical expertise and mobility of western hemisphere people. If you look at the distribution of corn from Central America halfway to the tip of Chile and halfway to the Arctic you start to get a bigger picture of pre-Columbian trade routes, geography, social interactions, city-states, and the sharing of agricultural expertise."[190]

Cradleboard's interactive, multimedia CD-ROM, *Science: Through Native American Eyes*, meets American National Content Standards for middle school science curriculum while addressing scientific concepts from within Native American cultures. *Science:*

Through Native American Eyes uses video, spoken word, animation, text, and music to study three concepts that most schools require at middle school level: the principles of friction, the science behind various kinds of human dwellings, in this case exemplified by Native American lodges, and the principles of sound. Although initially aimed at middle school grade reading levels, it is very usable by adults and even young children, much like television or video game viewers.

Like many of us, Buffy had always felt challenged to understand the concepts of frequency and amplitude that "just lie there on the page" as presented in books. She didn't complain about it: she fixed it. In studying frequency and amplitude in Cradleboard's "Principles of Sound" unit, multisensory lessons give children virtual hands-on access to interactive sliders, such as those used in music studios. Students can see the sound waves change in shape as they hear pitches get louder and softer in volume or higher and lower in pitch. More importantly, the students are in control of the interactive sliders themselves. Test scores improve greatly with this approach.

In "Principles of Friction," a Mohawk elder presents the traditional game of snow snake wherein a player hurls a long smooth lance down an icy track of sculpted snow. The stick has been smoothed in order to reduce friction. The lesson is reinforced by an interactive game of virtual snow snake in which the players play math games to compare speed scores.

Pueblo adobe houses, Plains tribe teepees, Great Lakes wigwams, and Iroquois longhouses are used for learning about the benefits and drawbacks of certain lodge styles and students come to understand why each group uses the lodge styles they do: for practical, survival-related, time-tested, and scientifically-explainable reasons.

Cradleboard includes free access to its online curriculum on social sciences and geography for elementary, middle, and high school grades. One high school geography unit broaches little-understood differences between the concepts of "sacred land" and "real estate":

"With the arrival of Europeans in the sixteenth century, the homelands of Native American people changed forever. A new concept about land was introduced for the first time in North America—the concept of land as "real estate," which is subject to ownership by an individual ... And thus, the taking of land from Native American people began with a vengeance and never stopped until very little land remained within Native American control. Even as tribes obtained guarantees from colonists and the U.S. government that certain pieces of land would belong to Aboriginal people forever, most agreements were broken unilaterally by the colonial governments, and more and more land was lost to Native American use ... By the end of the nineteenth century, very little of North America remained in Native American control. Even today, some tribes are still striving to maintain control of their lands, and to preserve those lands for future generations of their people."[191]

Buffy travelled widely on behalf of the Cradleboard project, spreading the message to teachers about Native American astronauts, pyramid cultures of the Americas, inventions, contributions to science, medicine, and agriculture. She pointed out the value in informing students (and sports fans) that the concept of team sport was invented by Native peoples of the Western Hemisphere, as was the rubber ball. This ability to use fascinating, "gee whiz" information about Native America further engages students in core learning via Cradleboard supplements.[192]

Teachers and students who use Cradleboard materials are often startled by the remarkable accomplishments of Native American peoples, including those associated with space exploration, medical research, and data-logging for Formula One racing. People are surprised to learn that lovingly wrapped Peruvian mummies pre-date Egyptian ones by more than 1000 years, and that ancient people in the Americas were using anesthesia, making dental crowns and fillings, and doing cranial surgery in pre-Columbian times.

Cradleboard also tackles racial prejudice and the attitudes that underlie it by directly engaging youth. The Nihewan Youth Council on Race focused on these issues through online chat rooms and discussion forums, providing a safe place for youth aged fourteen to twenty-one in which to define and discuss race issues with peers in other cultures worldwide.[193] Monetary awards were provided to participating Youth Council on Race students who shared their work through artistic/journalism projects of their own design.

Buffy overcame challenges in setting up the Cradleboard online programs. She had to search far and wide for a programmer who understood the technical requirements involved, and found Scott Flowers, who she then flew over to Hawaii. It took Flowers several months to complete the task.

Immediately upon Cradleboard's launch in 1996, reviews were spectacular. Teachers realized they finally had a valuable use for all the technology that they were learning about. There was not yet a lot of useful curriculum content on the Internet. The new Cradleboard paradigm went far beyond the specifics of its First Nations origins.

> "I am 13-years-old and I have been involved with the Cradleboard Project for two-and-a-half years. A lot of information and education has come from Cradleboard. And with the science curriculum CD, I learned how other Native cultures survive and what they believe. Cradleboard has opened a lot of doors of opportunity for me, which I am thankful for."
>
> *Mohawk student*

> "I have seen a lot of curriculum since I have been teaching, but nothing greater than this. I can actually relate to this curriculum more clearly than any other curriculum that I have evaluated."
>
> *Bellingham, Washington teacher candidate*

"I am quite a technophobe but was able to navigate my way through the set up instructions with relative ease. I also enjoy that there is a genuine utilization of culturally relevant material to convey important scientific principles."
Teacher, Ke Kaiapuni 'o' Anuenue School, Hawaii

"The Cradleboard Teaching Project. It speaks of hope, sharing, and cultural pride. Highly motivational."
Evaluation comment,
Native American Gifted and
Talented Conference Albuquerque, NM.

"What it does is to bring science into a human context that grounds the material for children. The challenge is that sometimes the science is lost. In this case, it is good science in the context of one people's culture."
Executive Director,
National Science Teachers Association

Keith Goulet, a prominent Aboriginal educator and Saskatchewan Minister of Education, the province where Buffy's roots are, presented her with a Distinguished Service Award in 2001 for her work in bringing the Cradleboard Teaching Project to the province. As well, the Cradleboard project was selected as one of more than 300 promising models identified by President Bill Clinton's "One America in the 21st Century: The President's Initiative on Race."

In 2008, Cradleboard achieved its mission of offering core curricula to the world for free via the Internet. Reducing Cradleboard's infrastructure was a major step, but clear thinking from the start had made it possible for the project to virtually run itself. The project now reaches thousands of classrooms worldwide. Buffy still has a very long wish list for Cradleboard, but that will have to wait for future fundraising and a launch into Phase Two, which will encompass even more educational materials and greater expansion of the classroom partnering program. Currently, Buffy's Nihewan Foundation is partnering with the Belinda Stronach Foundation's "One Laptop Per Child" initiative to bring thousands of free computers (embedded with excerpts from *Science through Native American Eyes*) to disadvantaged students across Canada.

Buffy gives much of the credit for the Cradleboard project's success in areas such as language to dedicated teachers: "I didn't get to be the one who taught elementary Cree to culture-deprived seven-year-olds, but something even better happened. Now we do have resurgence and a revitalizing of Indigenous languages. It's gone far beyond my wildest dreams of the 1950s and 1960s. From primary level Cree, all the way to contemporary college level teaching and learning, and even better into a broad and wide acceptance of expanding and supporting Indigenous languages and speakers in the real world. Now the dream is being implemented by true Cree speakers who were once ignored. So here's to dreaming.

"When it comes to envisioning, there's no such thing as biting off more than you can chew! ... We've come a long way in the past forty years, as friends and networks of classroom teachers, at the university level, PhDs, you know—warriors."

Buffy also appreciates the positives she sees in Canada: "The farther south you go in the Western Hemisphere, the worse it gets for Indigenous people. In Uruguay, there are few Indians—they were systematically eradicated. It was complete genocide. Chile is not a lot of fun either. In the United States there is no such thing as the Aboriginal Peoples' Television Network or yearly award shows celebrating Native American achievers. In my opinion, Canada is the best of the colonial lot. There's a long way to go, but at least we're going."

Musician Robbie Robertson appreciates the significance of what Buffy has achieved in music and in other initiatives. "You can't help but just cheer inside a little bit when somebody like Buffy stands up and says, 'Let me tell you something.' You think: this is the real thing, this is the real deal ... Somebody that comes from where she comes from ... you have to break through. It isn't like they've got the door open wide saying, 'Hey all you Indians, come in.' It isn't like that in the real world.

"So this girl had to stand up and break through barriers. And I'm proud that she's done it. In what she does, in who she is now, and that she walks the Earth: it's a good thing. What she has done and the contributions she has made and the way she has done it, it's always with a certain beauty and elegance in the way she has handled things. Even when some of the stuff is tough, there's something very classy in the way she's brought off her opinions."[194]

Danish television producer and college professor Stig Thornsohn knew Buffy from his teaching days in California where he, too, was an activist and friend to the American Indian Movement. He saw how the Indigenous peoples of North America had been broken up into isolated reservations in a divide-and-conquer principle. Thornsohn believes Buffy has turned the Internet into a sort of digital smoke signal, reconnecting all of these little islands of people again. If Cradleboard is a smoke signal, it is a very powerful one at that.[195]

CHAPTER 11

CONTINUING
TO RIPEN

＊

In 2009, Buffy released *Running for the Drum*, thirteen years after *Up Where We Belong*. She writes all the time and has all kinds of unrecorded songs, but Buffy only records when she's ready to tour. For *Running for the Drum*, again she called upon her friend and producer Chris Birkett who flew to Hawaii from France several times in order that the production could be done in Buffy's home studio. They co-produced *Running for the Drum*, as they had done *Coincidence and Likely Stories* and *Up Where We Belong*.

Before they began recording, Buffy presented Birkett with a cassette of eighteen demos she'd already made of new songs, complete with traditional powwow singing, electronic effects, and remix style loops that would have seemed unusual a decade earlier, and other original touches.

"I'm terrible at recording myself," Buffy says. "When I have a hot song in my head, I'll record on anything handy, just press the button and go while it's hot and fresh, never mind the crappy sound. But Chris is a master recordist, a great engineer, an emotional guitar and bass player, and a sensitive listener who hears my ideas and tries hard to capture what I do in demo mode. We like working together and that makes it wonderful."[196]

The finished *Running for the Drum* is very much like those original demos, with the addition of Birkett's bass and guitar parts, and contributions from a few select and original musicians in Hawaii and in Paris. Although most of *Running for the Drum* is new material, she rerecorded "Little Wheel Spin and Spin," the title song of her third album, because it still makes sense today. *Running for the Drum* contains a "whiplash collection" of powwow rock, country, techno-dance remix, jazz, rockabilly and, as usual, big love songs—as diverse in styles as each of her previous albums.

Buffy describes *Running for the Drum* as a snapshot album of her creative life. The sound of the drum represents the heartbeat of life in Indian country, the urge to dance, and the call to love, independence and activism.

"No, No Keshagesh" is the opening track. "Keshagesh" is a Cree word meaning "greedy guts" and at Piapot "that's what they named a little puppy who used to eat his own dinner and then wanted everybody else's, too." It is a metaphor for corporate greed and is directed towards bankers and war profiteers:

These old men they make their dirty deals.
Go in the back room and see what they can steal.
Talk about your beautiful and spacious skies.
It's about uranium; it's about the water rights.

Got Mother Nature on a luncheon plate.
They carve her up and call it real estate.
Want all the resources and all of the land
They make a war over it – Blow things up for it
The reservation out at Poverty Row
There's something cooking and the lights are low
Somebody's trying to save our Mother Earth
I'm gonna help em to save it and sing it and pray it
And say it singing
No no Keshagesh you can't do that no more.
"No No Keshagesh"

It's a serious song but "No No Keshagesh" is also a tune you can dance to. Similarly, "Working for the Government," despite its subject matter of government operatives who act like international James Bond-style mercenaries, has a dancey, techno, Euro-pop feel unfamiliar in Indian country.

When Buffy's nephew Rodney Obey, a traditional singer and drum maker, was a teenager, he used to travel to powwows with a tape recorder, sharing songs. One that he sent to Buffy included a group of kids singing in their own language. "I wrote a song around it but we couldn't figure out who it was that Rodney had taped. It turned out to be the Black Lodge Singers when they were kids, who went on to be one of the most beloved groups on the powwow circuit. I'd always loved them as adults, and their kids' songs are the best, and I was so thrilled to realize that they were the ones on the mystery tape I'd loved for twenty years. I contacted them, used their sample and turned it into "Cho Cho Fire," a real rocker, dedicated to jingle dress dancers."[197]

Other songs are heartfelt reminiscences that have emerged from Buffy's relationships with the Piapots and the Obeys. "Still This Love Goes On" is an acoustic tribute to reservation life, and comforts Buffy and the band when they're on the road: "In every dream I can smell the sweet grass burning and in my heart always hear the drum and hear the singers soaring, and see the jingle dancers, and still this love goes on and on and on."[198] *Running for the Drum* received several accolades, including a 2009 Juno Award.

Earlier, in 2006, CineFocus Canada, a Toronto production company owned by filmmakers Joan Prowse and John Bessai, joined with executive producer Gilles Paquin of Paquin Entertainment Group to create the highly acclaimed documentary, *Buffy Sainte-Marie: A Multimedia Life*. The ambitious documentary, directed by Prowse, was the first to capture the full range of Buffy's career as seen through the eyes of her family, friends, and contemporaries, especially in Canada. The DVD is included as a bonus in her 2008 album *Running for the Drum*.

Preparing to tour in support of *Running for the Drum* in 2009, Buffy auditioned musicians in Winnipeg and discovered an all-Aboriginal heavy metal band of musicians she describes as a "whack 'em, smack 'em, rock band" to provide the high-energy sound she was looking for. Band members Jesse Green, Leroy Constant, and Mike Bruyere know exactly what the environments reflected in so many of Buffy's songs are about. About the band, Buffy said: "They've got the energy I need for driving songs like 'Starwalker' and 'No No Keshagesh' and it helps that what I sing about and where a lot of my songs come from is a world they know too: the realities of Native American passion, love, tragedy and music."[199] Buffy and the band cut their teeth with appearances at local smaller venues where they could polish their show.

Buffy's *Running for the Drum* world tour got off to a roaring start in early 2010—taking the United Kingdom by storm, they played five cities in England and Scotland in the last six days of January.

The tour continued through mainland Europe, starting in Germany—North American Indian culture is huge there—with appearances in Hamburg, Berlin, Cologne, Brussels, Amsterdam, and Paris. One German fan showed up wearing an Indian headdress.

Europe set a hectic pace, driving from country to country in a van, checking into a different hotel every night: wake up, shower, eat, then go for sound check. If lucky, they would have a day off to take in some tourist sites. The group always prayed together before going on stage and met later to discuss each show. Following the performance and after-performance autograph sessions, if they didn't have a show the next night, they might go out dancing and have some fun. However, they were usually lucky to catch a bit of shut-eye before catching a 4 am flight to the next place. When Buffy was training the band for their first gruelling tour, she advised them that, "Doing one-nighters involves late nights, early mornings. You better sleep whenever you can, because you never know when you'll get another chance. It's an exhausting pace, and on top of it you have huge jet lag messing up your sleep. So you better be smart and take care of yourself. If you act like you're in Spinal Tap, you'll burn out and have to go home to Mama."[200]

"Attitude is so important," says Jesse Green. "Touring doesn't have to be viewed as a world of cut-throat competition. Every group is unique and should be respected for what they have to offer." Mike Bruyere plays a special role in the band. His family has taught him the importance of observing his Aboriginal spiritual traditions as a means of remaining grounded in the world so he carries traditional herbs like sweetgrass and sage. Before each performance, Buffy and the band set aside time to smudge (wave a burning bundle of herbs through the air to cleanse or purify an area or eliminate negativity) and pray that things go well. It helps them all to remain grounded by remembering their roots and where they came from. Thus spirituality plays an important part in touring. Through it all, Green, Bruyere, and the other band members found that Buffy treated them like family—easygoing and fun to be with.[201]

In a typical performance, Buffy begins with her signature song, "The Piney Wood Hills," alone, before bringing in the band on the second verse, and then blowing everyone away with a huge powwow rocker like "Cho Cho Fire." Songs about environmental greed and classics like "Until It's Time for You to Go" and "Up Where We Belong" are interspersed with rockabilly, country, and simple acoustic songs. Typically the show ends with "Bury My heart at Wounded Knee" and "Starwalker," leaving audiences shouting for more. Some Europeans had studied "Universal Soldier" as part of their school curriculum and fans were seen weeping when they heard the song in person because of the emotions it evoked.

Buffy and the band played in Paris on February 10, then quickly returned to Canada to perform at the Vancouver Olympics on February 12, playing under the effects of jet lag. Capping off the Canadian leg of the tour were appearances at the small town of Bengough and the Regina Folk Festival, both in Saskatchewan.

International touring can be gruelling and there has been no shortage of demand for Buffy's appearances. Her manager, Gilles Paquin, comes from a theatre background and has a genius for logistics and keeping a company of players on the road. With Buffy's help, the band has learned how to tour, play big-time international concerts without burning out, stay in shape, and always be ready for anything. Being on the road is like part of the show—there are certain roles and expectations. They've learned how to deal with agents, immigration, weird hours, road managers, and crews. A performer is looked up to and needs to be clear in terms of expectations.

For Buffy, 2011 proved to be another exciting international year. She wanted to do a benefit for her local public radio station in Hawaii and to thank the band for all the hard touring they'd been doing. Using her United Airlines miles (she is a Million Miler), Buffy brought the band to Hawaii for nine days. They did the benefit concert, raising about $17,000 for the station, and then hit the beach. To Jesse Green's surprise, Buffy took a surfboard out for a spin, and Green, Bruyere, and Constant discovered a new passion.

After their break, Buffy and the band flew to Australia, appearing at the National Theatre in Melbourne on April 20 and the State Theatre at Sydney on April 23. Then came the Byron Bay Bluesfest, where they played two consecutive nights to 22,000 people and where Buffy was able to spend some time with her old friend from Greenwich Village, Bob Dylan. While in Byron Bay, Buffy was also reunited with an old friend from Hawaii, world-renowned big wave surfer Rusty Miller, and the band got to catch a few more waves.

Buffy and the guys had planned on playing New Zealand but postponed after the massive earthquake that struck Christchurch in February. That summer they returned to England to hang out with James Blunt and Cyndi Lauper (Lauper and Buffy are mutual fans), before heading to Denmark and Norway (by boat, no less). Finally, it was back to Canada, where they played Bruyere's hometown, the Sagkeeng Reserve in Manitoba, and eventually played gigs in almost every province and territory.

Buffy's tour focused mainly on Europe and Canada, where her popularity has always been strong. Green observed that European audiences tend to be larger and emotionally more involved than American ones. The American stops were mainly major centres such as New York, Washington, and Los Angeles, though she also played smaller venues such as reservations where her American Indian fan base has always endured. Buffy recognizes that she will never be a top seller in the American market, with her career having been stymied at its most promising point, and that recovering that momentum is virtually impossible.

Toward the end of summer 2011, the tour skirted the west coast of the United States from Arlington, Washington, to Grass Valley and Oakland, California, before heading to the American Southwest, appearing in Albuquerque, Phoenix, and the Aguacaliente Reservation near Palm Springs.

The young band has come to accept the early morning risings to catch planes, but the excitement of the next stop is always exhilarating. The band members are amazed at how fit Buffy stays. Buffy finds running too monotonous, and reveals that one of her favourite ways of staying in shape is through her passion for flamenco dancing—any kind of dancing, actually. After their concerts, the band goes out as a group to burn off extra adrenaline on the dance floor. While in Hawaii, Buffy treated the band to a day in the gym with her personal trainer, Char Ravelo, and together they created a television segment about staying fit on the road. Buffy attributes her energy to regular workouts and hating the taste of alcohol.

Buffy has a significant legacy to protect. Without her permission, three of Buffy's obscure 1970s albums were re-released by a British company that believed the recordings were public domain and therefore unprotected. Fact-checking her contracts with MCA and ABC Records confirmed that, indeed, all three 1970s recordings reverted to Buffy after a certain period, and she let the British label know. They backed down, realizing they had no other choice, and Buffy released the material in 2010 on her label, Gypsy Boy Music, under the title *The Pathfinder: Buried Treasures*. "Of course, some of the recordings sound dated," she says, "but most of them I recorded with Norbert Putnam and the Area Code 615 band, and the songs were mostly real good, but they never got to be heard." Today, Buffy and her band introduce some of these strong, lost songs: "Sweet Little Vera," "Look at the Facts," and "Generation" with its prescient line, "Bye bye banker's trust."

Buffy's longevity in the music business, now approaching fifty years, is in itself amazing. Buffy reflects that she used to be really shy and focused only on the song. She began to reconsider her songwriter uniqueness as a special tool that would help her grow into a more effective performer. She continues to have a mission to be effective in making positive change where and when and however she can. In talking about Native issues, Buffy sees beyond racism, identifying the real villain as the quest for further power and greed on the part of the already powerful, whatever their race. Her approach has been a non-combative, non-judgmental one of understanding human problems as a result of the immaturity of our young species, which she maintains is still developing. "Seems like the human race is a work in progress," she says. "Each one of us is, and we're all ripening day by day."[202]

Buffy sees herself as an artist first, then a professional singer, educator, and activist. She wants to be remembered as an individual who discovered her inherent creativity as a little child and nurtured it in the face of significant obstacles—being female, or Native American, or living out of the loop in far-away Hawaii. Key to Buffy's success is that her creativity is pure—she never got involved with alcohol and has avoided hard drugs. She craves fresh food, spends her money on fresh juice instead of martinis, and maintains an active life leading a great band. When she's off the road, Buffy feeds on solitude and immersion in nature with plants and animals, enabling her to tap into this wellspring and continually rejuvenate. But lest one think that her success comes simply from an overflowing of creativity and talent, those who know Buffy are also aware of how hard and unceasingly she works. When she takes on a task, she invests 110 percent effort, underscoring the adage that success comes as much from perspiration as from inspiration.

Guitarist and music chronicler Randy Bachman observes that show business life isn't always glamorous. The artist is constantly travelling with the same entourage and that world becomes a very small circle. You can be alone every night, and most get sick of it after a while. The routine can affect your sanity and sometimes it is necessary to just get away from it all.[203]

Buffy admits that the journey has often been a lonely one. But she has come to appreciate the hidden power of being solitary. "I came to rely greatly on the part of me that was quite comfortable being private. And still I carry that today, even in airports when there is nobody I know. I travel, and in foreign countries I feel pretty comfortable. I don't feel lonely. I read and I write. I pray and I hear music in my head. I dream and I see visions of pictures that I can turn into paintings. More than that, I see visions in the intellectual side of myself, where words come together with music and pictures for me. I think it's very natural, like kids at the beach, and I treasure the gifts that have been my best friends ever since I was a child."[204]

Buffy is self-deprecating about many things. She sometimes works out to keep in shape, but once joked that the real way she keeps fit is by chasing goats and airplanes. Despite the drawbacks of frequent travel, she feels lucky to have had a life filled with plane tickets, as this has given her ample opportunity to observe people—rich and poor, city and rural, doing well and not doing so well. And this has taught her a lot. Buffy has never-ending optimism and joy, a real pleasure in meeting people and maintaining friendships. Developing and maintaining such connections and friendships over the years has required tremendous energy and sacrifice. Yet she has no plans to slow down. Buffy has often noted that her career path "is her way" and cautions that it is not an easy route for someone else to follow.

Despite being a star, Buffy has always treasured time with her relatives at Piapot, sharing both fun and tears, aware that they come from a great nation and are a great people. She is a role model and inspiration to communities where there are problems with alcohol and drugs, despair, and social problems.

Albert Angus admires her life choices: "Buffy has always been pretty successful in everything she does and as a result has gained respect. Here is an individual who has had such a high public profile, but who has never as far as I know made a mistake. Certainly nothing that is detrimental to her past or her career or her family. Everything has been so honourable in the things she does and a lot of people have learned from her. Whatever she does, she has my support."[205]

American Indian academics have contemplated Buffy's role in the nascent development of American Indian awareness: "Buffy has consistently devoted herself to revising both the public perception and real situation of her people on all levels ... Buffy has had an incalculable impact on the bulk of a generation of Indian youth ... Buffy's impact has hardly been restricted to influencing younger people who want to follow in her footsteps. The apparently spontaneous interface she achieved with other social elements was instrumental in establishing the environment that allowed the emergence of overtly political Native organizations such as the American Indian Movement (AIM) during the late 1960s."[206]

Robbie Robertson believes that Buffy will leave a significant legacy. "Fifty years, 200 years from now, Buffy's lyrics, Buffy's music will be remembered. She's done so many things she'll be remembered for being as complex and simple as she is. She has so many ways of saying the same thing, she has so many ways of singing about the beauty way, she has so many ways of raising awareness. So the power of it is the combined power of the many things she has done."[207]

Back home in Hawaii, you might find Buffy standing in front

of an easel on her wooden deck overlooking her goat pasture, with towering Norfolk pines lined up in the background and massive green peaks in the distance. Vines with pretty pink, bell-shaped flowers hang along the side of the house. She may be painting images of goats in unusual green and purple hues. Meanwhile, you can hear the rain in the pastures and on the roof.

Buffy enthusiastically campaigned for Barack Obama and reacted with understandable joy the night he was elected President of the United States in November, 2008. She was thrilled that finally a professor of constitutional law occupied the White House. She is inspired by Obama's great qualifications and wonderful temperament and is proud to have campaigned for his election.

Hawaii was much quieter when Buffy first arrived in 1967 and has become much more crowded and difficult for Indigenous people. It runs the danger, she says, of becoming like a "big T-shirt shop in the real estate market." Still, Buffy "finds the spiritual" in the forests and vegetation. She continues to deeply enjoy the company of her goats, her cat, and two retired horses, all from the local rescue shelter.

Buffy cared for her mother Winifred until Winifred's death in 2010. Buffy's son, Cody, is a filmmaker and a keyboard player in several reggae bands, intent on making his own mark as a unique individual. Buffy feels blessed to still be in touch with her friend from college, Taj Mahal, who lived not far from her in Hawaii from 1981 to 2005. Cody has a close bond with the Mahal kids, and Inshirah Mahal, their mother, is close to Buffy.

While Buffy has received accolades for her music, it has not been until recently that she received substantial public recognition for her endless efforts working with Aboriginal communities. Even in the AIM years of the 1970s, she stepped back and preferred to let others have the spotlight. From the 1980s to the present, Buffy's Cradleboard Teaching Project, which pioneered interactive, online education "through Native American eyes," is mainly known to educators and their students. Her philanthropic work, dating back to the Nihewan Foundation in 1968, has gone on largely unheralded except by charitable foundations, probably because of Buffy's own modesty and preference not to be in the spotlight simply for publicity's sake. Moreover, she has accomplished her goals mainly on her own initiative, without the benefit of government aid, and often to her own inconvenience. Still she has never grown tired, discouraged, cynical, or jaded, and feels that her mission is far from done:

"We all make our little contributions when we can and things change a little bit at a time. I think that's what ripens life. But it always seems so slow when you're carrying this Medicine and you know it can make things better, but there are gatekeepers profiting on the problems, and you'll have to wait awhile until the world is ready to receive it; so you go bit by bit: give when you have the chance.

"It's futile to try to rush the river, and pretty hard to hurry the moon, and sometimes you have to be content to plant good seeds whenever you can and be patient as you watch them grow and ripen.

Buffy's son, Cody (seen here with Buffy), is a filmmaker and a
keyboard player in several reggae bands.

Thinking about my early attempts to be effective, I can say that in
my lifetime things have not changed nearly enough; but when I
look back on the last forty years, things have changed incredibly
and I have great faith that the world will continue to ripen."[208]

ENDNOTES

1   *Native North American Biography,* Malinowsy & Glickman.

2   Canadian Broadcasting Corporation (CBC), "Bright Lights," February 24, 1969.

3   Dr. Martha Henry, interviewed by Blair Stonechild, November 14, 2007.

4   "Wakefield History," Wakefield Historical Commission.

5   Lainey Sainte-Marie, personal communication, December 7, 2007.

6   Ibid.

7   CineFocus-Paquin Pictures, *Buffy Sainte-Marie: A Multimedia Life,* 2006.

8   Buffy Sainte-Marie, interview by Blair Stonechild, May 18, 2005.

9   CBC, *Adrienne Clarkson Presents,* 1993.

10 Ibid.

11 *Today,* "Beginnings: Buffy Sainte-Marie."

12 Buffy Sainte-Marie, interview by Blair Stonechild, May 18, 2005.

13 *Today,* "Beginnings: Buffy Sainte-Marie."

14 Buffy Sainte-Marie, notes to Blair Stonechild.

15 Buffy Sainte-Marie, interview by Rodger Collins, 1996.

16 Today, "Beginnings: Buffy Sainte-Marie."

17 Ibid.

18 Buffy Sainte-Marie, notes to Blair Stonechild.

19 Janice Palumbo, personal communication with author, December 6, 2007.

20 Buffy Sainte-Marie, notes to Blair Stonechild.

21 CineFocus-Paquin Pictures, research interview for *Buffy Sainte-Marie: A Multimedia Life.*

22 CineFocus-Paquin Pictures, *Buffy Sainte-Marie: A Multimedia Life.*

23 Ibid., interview with Buffy Sainte-Marie.

24 *Saskatoon Star-Phoenix,* "Buffy Soldiers on for kids."

25 Ibid.

26   Buffy Sainte-Marie, notes to Blair Stonechild.

27   Beebe Library, Wakefield, Massachusetts.

28   www.bayrdstradingpost.com

29   Buffy Sainte-Marie, interview by Blair Stonechild, May 18, 2005.

30   CBC, *Bright Lights*, February 24, 1969.

31   Ibid.

32   CineFocus-Paquin Pictures, research interview for *Buffy Sainte-Marie: A Multimedia Life*.

33   Buffy Sainte-Marie, interview by Blair Stonechild, October 12, 2007.

34   CineFocus-Paquin Pictures, research interview for *Buffy Sainte-Marie: A Multimedia Life*.

35   Cinefocus-Paquin Pictures, *Buffy Sainte-Marie: A Multimedia Life*.

36   *Time Magazine*, "Solitary Indian."

37   Buffy Sainte-Marie, interview by Blair Stonechild, October 12, 2007.

38   Denise Sullivan, "Buffy Sainte-Marie: Still Singing for Peace," *Crawdaddy*.

39   Buffy Sainte-Marie, notes to Blair Stonechild.

40   CBC, *Bright Lights*, February 24, 1969.

41   CBC, TBA, October 28, 1966.

42   CineFocus-Paquin Pictures, research interview for *Buffy Sainte-Marie: A Multimedia Life*.

43   Ibid.

44   CineFocus-Paquin Pictures, research interview for *Buffy Sainte-Marie: A Multimedia Life*.

45   Ibid.

46   CBC, *Bright Lights*, February 24, 1969.

47   *Life Magazine*, "Buffy's Many Voices."

48   Brenda George, interview by Blair Stonechild, October 3, 2008.

49   *Starweek Magazine*, "Starwoman."

50   CineFocus-Paquin Pictures, *Buffy Sainte-Marie: A Multimedia Life*.

51   CBC, *As It Happens*, November 7, 1977.

52   Rotolo, *A Freewheeling Time*, 273.

53   CineFocus-Paquin Pictures, *Buffy Sainte-Marie: A Multimedia Life.*

54   Van Ronk, *The Mayor of MacDougall Street*, 144.

55   Ibid, 147.

56   Rotolo, 228.

57   Peter La Farge, "Buffy Sainte-Marie," *Sing Out!*

58   CineFocus-Paquin Pictures, *Buffy Sainte-Marie: A Multimedia Life*, 2006.

59   Robert Shelton, "An Indian Girl Sings her Compositions and Folk Songs," *New York Times.*

60   Wikipedia – Vanguard Records, August 2007.

61   Maynard Solomon liner notes to *Its My Way*, Vanguard Records, 1964.

62   *Moonshot*, Vanguard Records.

63   CineFocus-Paquin Pictures, *Buffy Sainte- Marie: A Multimedia Life.*

64   Ibid.

65   *Life Magazine*, "Buffy's Many Voices."

66   Van Ronk, 174.

67   *Life Magazine*, "Buffy's Many Voices."

68   CineFocus-Paquin Pictures, interview with Buffy Sainte-Marie.

69   Ibid.

70   Ibid.

71   Ibid.

72   CineFocus-Paquin Pictures, interview with Buffy Sainte-Marie.

73   Nat Hentoff liner notes to *Little Wheel Spin and Spin*, Vanguard, 1966.

74   Heylin, *Bob Dylan: Behind the Shades*, 367.

75   Sainte-Marie, *The Buffy Sainte-Marie Songbook*, 130.

76   Ibid.

77   CineFocus-Paquin Pictures, interview with Buffy Sainte-Marie.

78   Buffy Sainte-Marie, interview by Blair Stonechild, May 18, 2005.

79   Buffy Sainte-Marie, notes to Blair Stonechild.

80   Ibid.

81   http://www.creative-native.com/index.htm.

82   Buffy Sainte-Marie, notes to Blair Stonechild.

83   Paul Barnsley, "Buffy Sainte-Marie and Elementary Teachers of Toronto," *Windspeaker*.

84   Delia Opekokew, interview with Blair Stonechild, Saskatoon, April 25, 2005.

85   Ibid.

86   Ibid.

87   Albert Angus, interview by Blair Stonechild, Calgary, May 12, 2005.

88   *Zoo World*, "As Many Buffys as There are Days."

89   Buffy Sainte-Marie, notes to Blair Stonechild.

90   Ibid.

91   Vanguard Records, *It's My Way!*

92   Buffy Sainte-Marie, interviewed by John Einarsen, July 1, 2004.

93   *ZooWorld*, June 20, 1974.

94   Buffy Sainte-Marie, personal commentary to author, May 20, 2010.

95   *San Francisco Chronicle*, "Buffy is a singer who can swing."

96   Buffy Sainte-Marie, notes to Blair Stonechild.

97   CineFocus-Paquin Pictures, interview with Buffy Sainte-Marie.

98   *Globe and Mail*, April 12, 1975.

99   Buffy Sainte-Marie, notes to Blair Stonechild.

100   Ibid.

101   Buffy Sainte-Marie, interview by Blair Stonechild, June 8, 2009.

102   CBC, *Metronome*, February 18, 1967.

103   CBC, *Bright Lights*, February 24, 1969.

104   CBC, *Metronome*, February 18, 1967.

105   CineFocus-Paquin Pictures, interview with Buffy Sainte-Marie.

106   Sainte-Marie, 1971.

107   CineFocus-Paquin Pictures, interview with Buffy Sainte-Marie.

108   Ibid.

109   CineFocus-Paquin Pictures, interview with Buffy Sainte-Marie.

110   Ibid., interview with Robbie Robertson.

111   Ibid., interview with Randy Bachman.

112   Ibid., interview with Tom Jackson by John Einarson.

113 Ibid.

114 Buffy Sainte-Marie, "Leonard Cohen ... His Songs," *Sing Out!*

115 Buffy Sainte-Marie, interview by Blair Stonechild, May 18, 2005.

116 "Mouthbows to Cyberskins," tribute site on Buffy Sainte-Marie.

117 buffysainte-marie.co.uk, a British tribute site.

118 CBC, *As it Happens*, November 7, 1977.

119 CineFocus-Paquin Pictures, *Buffy Sainte-Marie: A Multimedia Life*.

120 CBC, *TBA*, October 28, 1966.

121 President George Washington, Proclamation to Chief Cornplanter of the Senecas, December 29, 1790.

122 Sainte-Marie, 154.

123 Buffy Sainte-Marie, notes to Blair Stonechild.

124 CBC Radio, *Matinee*, July 24, 1970.

125 CBC, *TBA*, October 28, 1966.

126 CBC, *Bright Lights*, February 24, 1969.

127 *UCLA Daily Bruin*, October 14, 1970.

128 Smith and Warrior, *Like a Hurricane*, 28.

129 Ibid, 235.

130 CBC, *TBA*, October 28, 1966; and *Bright Lights*, February 24, 1969.

131 *Los Angeles Herald Examiner*, "Buffy Sainte-Marie: songs with a positive message."

132 *Longest Walk*, 1976.

133 CineFocus-Paquin Pictures, interview with Floyd "Red Crow" Westerman.

134 Ibid.

135 Sainte-Marie, 155.

136 Los Angeles Times Free Press, "Buffy Sainte-Marie on the American Indian."

137 Longest Walk, 1976, see www.longestwalk.org.

138 Ward Churchill, Mary Ann Hill and Norbert Hill, Jr., "Examination of Stereotyping: An Analytical Survey of Twentieth-Century Indian Entertainers," in Bataille et al, The Pretend Indians, 364.

139 CineFocus-Paquin Pictures, *Buffy Sainte-Marie: A Multimedia Life*.

140   www.informationliberation.com.

141   Buffy Sainte-Marie, comments to Blair Stonechild, March 2010.

142   CineFocus-Paquin Pictures, interview with Charlie Hill.

143   CineFocus-Paquin Pictures, interview with Curtis Jonnie.

144   CineFocus-Paquin Pictures, interview with Charlie Hill.

145   CineFocus-Paquin Pictures, interview with Curtis Jonnie.

146   Ibid.

147   Ibid.

148   Ibid., interview with Charlie Hill.

149   CineFocus-Paquin Pictures, interview with Buffy Sainte-Marie.

150   Ibid.

151   CineFocus-Paquin Pictures, interview with Buffy Sainte-Marie.

152   Ibid.

153   www.creative-native.com, "Digital Art Interview."

154   Soraya Peebaye, "Multi-Media Child: Buffy Sainte-Marie," www.cyberstage.org.

155   CBC, *This Morning*, February 1, 2002.

156   Howard Rheinhold, "Folk Songs, Digital Art and Indian Empowerment," *San Francisco Chronicle*.

157   Peebaye, 1.

158   www.creative-native.com, "Digital art interview."

159   Buffy Sainte-Marie, notes to Blair Stonechild.

160   Buffy Sainte-Marie, "Cyberskins," at www.creative-native.com.

161   Buffy Sainte-Marie, interview by Blair Stonechild, October 12, 2007.

162   CineFocus-Paquin Pictures, interview with Buffy Sainte-Marie.

163   Ibid.

164   CineFocus-Paquin Pictures: *Buffy Sainte-Marie: A Multimedia Life.*

165   CineFocus-Paquin Pictures, interview with Buffy Sainte-Marie.

166   Ibid.

167   Buffy Sainte-Marie, notes to Blair Stonechild.

168   CBC, *Our Native Land*, December 29, 1984.

169   CineFocus-Paquin Pictures, interview with Buffy Sainte-Marie.

170 Buffy Sainte-Marie, notes to Blair Stonechild.

171 CineFocus-Paquin Pictures, interview with Chris Birkett.

172 Buffy Sainte-Marie, notes to Blair Stonechild.

173 CineFocus-Paquin Pictures, interview with Robbie Robertson.

174 Ibid., interview with Chris Birkett.

175 Ibid., interview with Neil Chapman.

176 Ibid., interview with Elaine Bomberry.

177 Ibid.

178 CineFocus-Paquin Pictures, *Buffy Sainte-Marie: A Multimedia Life.*

179 Ibid.

180 Ibid., interview with Elaine Bomberry.

181 "Cradleboard History" at www.cradleboard.org.

182 Buffy Sainte-Marie, notes to Blair Stonechild.

183 "Cradleboard History."

184 Saskatchewan Indian Cultural Centre, Aboriginal Faces of Saskatchewan at www.sicc.sk.ca/faces/.

185 American Indian Program Council, "Cradleboard Project."

186 Kellogg Foundation, interview with Buffy Sainte-Marie, 2003.

187 Buffy Sainte-Marie, notes to Blair Stonechild.

188 Kellogg Foundation, interview with Buffy Sainte-Marie.

189 CineFocus-Paquin Pictures, interview with Buffy Sainte-Marie.

190 www.cradleboard.org

191 Ibid.

192 Kellogg Foundation, interview with Buffy Sainte-Marie.

193 Buffy Sainte-Marie, "Beyond Autumn's Stereotypes," presentation to American Indian Program Council.

194 CineFocus-Paquin Pictures, interview with Robbie Robertson.

195 CineFocus-Paquin Pictures, interview with Stig Thornsohn.

196 Buffy Sainte-Marie, notes to Blair Stonechild.

197 Buffy Sainte-Marie, notes to Blair Stonechild.

198 Buffy Sainte-Marie, "Still This Love Goes On" lyrics.

199   Buffy Sainte-Marie, www.creative-native.com.

200   Buffy Sainte-Marie, notes to Blair Stonechild.

201   Jesse Green, interview by Blair Stonechild, Winnipeg, September 12, 2011.

202   Buffy Sainte-Marie, notes to Blair Stonechild.

203   CineFocus-Paquin Pictures, interview with Randy Bachman.

204   Buffy Sainte-Marie, interview by Blair Stonechild, Saskatoon, May 18, 2005.

205   Albert Angus, interview by Blair Stonechild, 2005.

206   Churchill, Hill and Hill, Jr., "Examination of Stereotyping," *The Pretend Indians*.

207   CineFocus-Paquin Pictures, interview with Robbie Robertson.

208   Ibid.

BIBLIOGRAPHY

BOOKS

Bataille, Gretchen and Charles Silet, *The Pretend Indians: Images of Native Americans in the Movies*. Iowa State University Press, 1980.

Brand, Johanna, *The Life and Death of Anna Mae Aquash,* Lorimer & Company, Toronto, 1978.

Callwood, June, *June Callwood's National Treasures*, Vision TV, Toronto, 1994.

Canadian Plains Research Centre, *Encyclopedia of Saskatchewan*, Regina, 2005.

Contemporary Canadian Musicians Issue 2 (Toronto 1998)

Churchill, Linda, *45 Profiles in Modern Music*, Weston Walch, 1996.

Churchill, Ward and Jim Vander Wall, *Agents of Repression: The FBI's Secret Wars Against the Black Panther Party and American Indian Movement*, South End Press, Boston, 1990.

Encyclopedia of Music in Canada

Goodwin, Doris K., *Lyndon Johnson and the American Dream*, St. Martin's Press, New York, 1976.

Gitlin, Todd, *The Sixties: Years of Hope, Days of Rage*, Bantam Books, 1987.

Hajdu, David, *Positively 4th Street*, Farrar, Straus and Giroux, New York, 2001.

Hale, Barrie. 'The Rebirth of Buffy Sainte-Marie,' *The Canadian*, 14 Jan 1978.

Helmsing, Jeffery, *Johnson's War; Johnson's Great Society*, Praeger publishers, Westport, Connecticutt, 2000.

Heylin, Clinton, *Bob Dylan: Behind the Shades*, Penguin Books, New York, 2001

Hitchcock, Wiley and Stanley Sadie, *New Grove Dictionary of American Music*, MacMillan, 1986.

Jeuttner, Bonnie, *100 American Indians: Who Shaped American History*, Bluewood Books, San Mateo, 2002.

Johnson, Troy, Joane Nagel and Duane Champagne, *American Indian Activism: Alcatraz to the Longest Walk*, University of Illinois Press, Chicago, 1997.

Katz, Jane B., *I am the Fire of Time*, Clarke, Irwin & Company, Toronto, 1977.

Koppe, Victoria, "Driven by Dancing Gods and Bathtub Whales," in Sainte-Marie, Buffy, *The Buffy Sainte-Marie Songbook*, Grosset & Dunlap, New York, 1971.

Malinowsky, Sharon & Simon Glickman (eds), *Native North American Biography*, Gale Group, 1996.

Means, Russell with Marvin Wolf, *Where White Men Fear to Tread: The Autobiography of Russell Means*, St. Martin Griffins, New York, 1995

Mercer, Michelle, *Will You Take Me as I Am: Joni Mitchell's Blue Period*, Simon & Shuster, 2009

Miller, Mark, "Sainte-Marie, Buffy (Beverley)," in Helmut Kallman et al. (eds) *Encyclopedia of Music in Canada*. Toronto: University of Toronto Press, 1992 (second edition).

Rotolo, Suze, *A Freewheelin Time: A Memoir of Greenwich Village in the Sixties*, Broadway Books, New York, 2008.

Sainte-Marie, Buffy, *The Buffy Sainte-Marie Songbook*, Grosset & Dunlap, New York, 1971.

Sainte-Marie, Buffy, *Nokusis and the Magic Hat*, 1986.

Shevey, Sandra, *Ladies of Pop/Rock*, Scholastic Book Services, 1971.

Smith, Paul and Robert Allan Warrior, *Like a Hurricane: The Indian Movement from Alcatraz to Wounded Knee*, The New Press, New York, 1996.

Stambler, Irwin and Grelun Landon, *Encyclopedia of Folk, Country and Western Music*, St. Martins, 1969.

Tudor, Dean, *Popular Music: An Annotated Guide to Recordings*, Libraries Unlimited, 1983.

Nygaard King, Betty, "Buffy Sainte-Marie," *The Canadian Encyclopedia*.

Van Ronk, Dave, *The Mayor of MacDougall Street*, De Capo Press, Cambridge, 2005.

Watetch, Abel, *Payepot and His People*, Canadian Plains Research Centre, Regina, 1997.

INTERVIEWS

Albert Angus interview by Blair Stonechild, Calgary, May 12, 2005.

Bordeaux, Lionel, Sinte Gleska University, South Dakota, phone interview with Blair Stonechild, December 11, 2008.

Cinefocus-Paquin Pictures
- Anderson, Erik
- Bachman Randy
- Bomberry, Elaine
- Birkett, Chris
- Goulet, Keith
- Mitchell, Joni
- Piapot, Debbie
- Robertson, Robbie
- Sainte-Marie, Buffy
- Westerman, Floyd
- Wilson, Chuck

Henry, Dr. Martha, Centre for Adoption Research, University of Massachusetts Medical School, Boston, interview by Blair Stonechild, November 14, 2007.

Hill, Charlie, "Club Red," Los Angeles, phone interview with Blair Stonechild, 2007.

Mancuzo, Sonia, Sesame Street Workshop, New York, interview by Blair Stonechild, 2005.

Opekokew, Delia, interview by Blair Stonechild, Saskatoon, April 25, 2005.

Palumbo, Janice, N. H., interview by Blair Stonechild, December 15, 2007.

Buffy Sainte-Marie, Interviews by Blair Stonechild, Saskatoon, May 18, 2005, Regina, February 10 and November 1, 2006, October 12, 2007, November 14, 2007, December 10, 2008, June 8, 2009, and various communications.

Sainte-Marie, Buffy, various interviews:
- *TBA*, CBC, October 28, 1966.
- interview on *CBC Metronome*, February 18, 1967.
- interview on *Bright Lights*, February 24, 1969.
- interview on *Matinee*, July 24, 1970.
- interview on *As It Happens*, November 7, 1977.
- interview on *Our Native Land*, December 29, 1984.
- CBC, "Midday," August 15, 1988.
- CBC, Buffy at Fort Qu'Appelle Powwow, 1993
- CBC, "Friday Night with Ralph Benmurgi," January 22, 1993.
- telephone interview by Rodger Collins, 1996.
- interview on *This Morning*, February 1, 2002.
- interview for W.K. Kellogg Foundation, May 2003.
- interview by Joseph Roberts, *Common Ground*, March 2005.

- interview by Vicki Gabereau, CBC Radio, March 26, 2005.
- "Digital Art Interview" on www.creative-native .com

Sainte-Marie, Lainey, Arlington, MA., interview by Blair Stonechild, December 12, 2007.

Woods, Patricia, interview by Blair stonechild, Amherst, Massachusetts

George, Brenda, interview by Blair Stonechild, Regina, SK. October 3, 2008.

Goulet, Keith, Regina, personal communication

Rose, Len, Wilmington, Massachusetts, December 2007

Tootoosis, Tyrone, Saskatoon, personal communication

NEWSPAPER ARTICLES

New York Times, "An Indian girl sings her compositions and folk songs," by Robert Shelton, August 17, 1963.

San Francisco Chronicle, "Buffy and other Berkeley sounds," May 26, 1969.

San Francisco Chronicle, "Buffy's a singer who can swing," June 8, 1969.

The Philadelphia Evening Bulletin, "To correct lies in history books," July 22, 1969

Globe and Mail, "Buffy an appealing, articulate spokesman," March 16, 1970.

UCLA Bruin, "Buffy Sainte-Marie, "Conquering myths of the Old West," October 14, 1970

Los Angeles Free Press, "Buffy Sainte-Marie on the American Indian," January 1, 1971.

Variety, "Concert Review: Hunter College, N.Y.," July 7, 1971.

Los Angeles Herald-Examiner, "Buffy Sainte-Marie: songs with a positive message," April 11, 1972.

Los Angeles Times, "One-woman show by Buffy Sainte-Marie," June 6, 1972,

Chicago Daily News, "Strong Songs by Buffy Sainte-Marie," June 29, 1972,

Toronto Star, "Sainte-Marie concert a throw-back to the '60s," March 21, 1975.

Globe and Mail, "Buffy Sainte-Marie: a five drum performance for our native royalty," November 11, 1977.

Globe and Mail, Kelly, M.J. "Halfway around the world for a free concert Buffy comes back to Toronto," 22 Dec 1986

Toronto Star, "Buffy Goes to bat for unlikely hero," February 1, 1989.

Toronto Star, "Buffy's back with first album in 15 years," March 17, 1992.

Globe and Mail, "Buffy Sainte-Marie to be in Hall of Fame," November 4, 1994.

San Francisco Chronicle, Rheingold, Howard, "Folk Songs, Digital Art and Indian Empowerment," 1994

Globe and Mail, Ross, Val. 'Buffy's sound and light show,' Toronto, May 19, 1995

Christian Science Monitor, June 21, 1995, "Program Brings Native American Culture to Schools," by Carol Berger

Times, London, England, February 16, 1996.

Calgary Sun, "Magic follows Sainte-Marie," August 21, 1996,

Hamilton Spectator, "Buffy Sainte-Marie inducted into Juno Hall of Fame," March 23, 1997.

Philadelphia Inquirer, "Net seeks to offer accurate view of Native American cultures." By Joyce K. Valenza, April 30, 1998.

Milwaukee Journal Sentinel, "Smithsonian pays homage to 'Broadside' folk anthems," July 2, 2000.

Saskatoon Star-Phoenix, "Buffy soldiers on for kids," in September 23, 2003.

Huffington Post, Ragogna, Mike, "An interview with Buffy Sainte-Marie," Aug. 13, 2009.

MAGAZINE ARTICLES

American Indian Review, Issue Number 3, Spring 1992, "Buffy Sainte-Marie."

Billboard, June 13, 1992.

Buffy Sainte-Marie: Up Where We Belong. CBC Home Video; 1996.

Education Week Magazine, October 27, 1999.

High Fidelity, August 1974.

Indian Country Today, Norrell, Brenda, "Buffy Sainte-Marie's censored sounds," August 5, 2006.

Let it Rock, Gray, Michael, "The Best of Buffy Sainte-Marie," June 1974.

Life Magazine, December 10, 1965.

Los Angeles Business Journal, "Names under the sun: Buffy Sainte-Marie – multi awarded Native American singer makes a comeback" May, 1992,

Maclean's Magazine, "Songs that Soar," April 20, 1992.

Melody Maker, Charlesworth, Chris, "Buffy Beaks Away," July, 1974.

NME, Murray, Charles Shaar, "Buffy Sainte-Marie: Never Argue with a Pregnant Indian," April, 1976.

Ms. Magazine, Edut, Ophira, "Buffy's New Gigabyte," August 1999.

"Now," "Politics Temper Tunes of the Heart, April 14, 1988.

Peebaye, Soraya, "Multi-Media Child: Buffy Sainte-Marie," 1996.

People, June 17, 1996.

Prochak, Michael, "Home is where Buffy's Art Is"

Rolling Stone, April 25, 1974 and November 26, 1992.

RPM, McLean, Steve. 'Buffy Sainte-Marie back with new album after 16 years,' April 4, 1992.

The Beat Magazine, Gowling, Ralph, "Buffy's catalogues spell success," November 2010.

Time Magazine, "Solitary Indian," December 10, 1965.

Today newsmagazine, "Beginnings: Buffy Sainte-Marie", February 7, 1981.

Toronto Now, Jung, Daryl, "Politics temper tunes of the heart," February 7, 1981.

Sesame Street Parents Magazine, May 2000.

Sing Out!, LaFarge, Peter, "Buffy Sainte-Marie," 1965.

Starweek Magazine, "Star Woman," September 3, 1981.

USA Today, "Science Through Native American Eyes," December 12, 2000.

Winds of Change Magazine, Sainte-Marie, B., 'Science, Creativity and Leadership,' spring 2001

Wired Online Magazine, "Sharing the Fire Online" by Steve Silberman, June 1, 1998.

Zoo World Magazine, "As Many Buffys as There are Days," June 20, 1974.

OTHER MEDIA

British tribute site, www.buffysaintemarie.co.uk/

Buffy Sainte-Marie website: www.creative-native.com

Buffy Sainte-Marie Cradleboard Website www.cradleboard.org

"Buffy Sainte-Marie" in www.Wikipedia.org

Discussion site http://launch.groups.yahoo.com/group/buffysaintemarie/

Netherlands tribute site, www.cshvof.com/buffy/

Nihewan Foundation Website www.nihewan.org

"The Longest Walk" CD at longestwalk.org

U. S. tribute site, "Mouth-bows to Cyberskin," www.mouth-bow.org

W. K. Kellogg Foundation, *A Culture of Giving: Service-Learning in Native American Communities* (Video) 2003.

ABOUT THE AUTHOR

Dr. Blair Stonechild is a member of the Muscowpetung First Nation in Saskatchewan. He obtained his B.A. from McGill, and M.A. and Ph.D. degrees from the University of Regina, and in 1976 was the first academic hired by the Saskatchewan Indian Federated College (SIFC). Blair is currently Professor of Indigenous Studies and has served as Dean of Academics and Executive Director of Development for the First Nations University of Canada (formerly Saskatchewan Indian Federated College). He co-authored with Dr. Bill Waiser, *Loyal Till Death: Indians and the North-West Rebellion*, which won the Saskatchewan Book Award and was a finalist for the Governor General's Literary Award in 1997. Dr. Stonechild's book on First Nations post-secondary policy, *The New Buffalo: Aboriginal Post-secondary Policy in Canada* (2006), was a finalist for the Saskatchewan Book Award. Blair was a Trustee of the Canadian Museum of Civilization from 1990 to 1998. He has done extensive consulting on Aboriginal education. Blair is married to Sylvia and is father to Michael, Rachel, and Gabrielle.

CREDITS

IMAGES

Cover — Photo by Denise Grant; from the Buffy Sainte-Marie collection

Pg. 5 — Photo from the Buffy Sainte-Marie collection

Pg. 49 — Photo courtesy of Lorne Stephenson; from the Buffy Sainte-Marie collection

Pg. 5 — Photo from the Buffy Sainte-Marie collection

Pg. 54 — Photo from the Buffy Sainte-Marie collection

Pg. 82 — Photo from the Buffy Sainte-Marie collection

Pg. 107 — Album cover from Vanguard Records; from the Buffy Sainte-Marie collection

Pg. 113 — Album cover from Vanguard Records; from the Buffy Sainte-Marie collection

Pg. 132 — Photo from the Buffy Sainte-Marie collection

Pg. 166 — Photo from the Buffy Sainte-Marie collection

Pg. 169 — Photo from the Buffy Sainte-Marie collection

Pg. 175 — Photo from the Children's Television Workshop; from the Buffy Sainte-Marie collection

Pg. 180 — Photo from the Buffy Sainte-Marie collection

Pg. 187 — Photo from the Buffy Sainte-Marie collection

Pg. 196 — Photo from the Buffy Sainte-Marie collection

Pg. 202 — Photo from the Buffy Sainte-Marie collection

Pg. 206 — Photo from the Buffy Sainte-Marie collection

Pg. 222 — Photo from the Buffy Sainte-Marie collection

Pg. 229 — Photo from the Buffy Sainte-Marie collection

Pg. 259 — Photo from the Buffy Sainte-Marie collection

LYRICS

INDEX